BACK TO BASICS: PLANNING

BACK TO BASICS: PLANNING

Mary Jean Parson
with
Matthew J. Culligan

Facts On File Publications
New York, New York ● Oxford, England

Back to Basics: Planning

Library of Congress Cataloging in Publication Data

Parson, Mary Jean, 1934
Back to basics: planning.
1. Planning. 2. Corporate planning. I. Culligan,
Matthew J. II. Title.
HD30.28.C84 1985 658.4'012 84-1582
ISBN O-8160-1057-9

Printed in the United States of America

10   9   8   7   6   5   4   3   2   1

Composition by Facts On File/Circle Graphics
Printed by R.R. Donnelley & Sons Co.

For
Muriel

CONTENTS

ACKNOWLEDGMENTS

My experience with learning the basics and philosophy of good business planning and then implementing it on a corporate and division level was typical of the vast majority of American middle-level managers who have found themselves in a highly competitive business that needed formal goals and strategies—it was on-the-job training.

Since I began the adventure of planning in 1970, I have read hundreds of thousands of words on the subject, trying to play "catch-up" with the formally trained MBAs who now populate the business world. But the bulk of the information in this book came from the actual experience of planning—of doing it and doing it and doing it, with the encouragement, knowledge and assistance of some very special people.

Robert T. Goldman introduced me to the philosophy and focus of planning, while Curtis Battles helped formalize the process. John Campbell, Ellis Moore and Walter Schwartz allowed me to experiment and to learn the analysis and implementation process on a division level. Michael A. Winter taught me the business-school techniques and procedures with the patience that only a good friend and colleague could demonstrate. Patty Gilhooly and Carol House took the ideas and strategies of business planning and translated them into detailed formulas, procedures and financial plans that worked. The Yale School of Drama welcomed the idea of introducing a planning course for its arts administration majors, and the outline for this book was born. Four years, forty students and many guest lecturers later, that outline has been "fleshed out" for managers, like me, who need to know why to plan, how to plan, and whether or not planning works.

The errors and misstatements in this book are all mine; the enthusiasm and encouragement came from those who have helped me, dedicated business professionals all. I thank them for their contribution.

Muriel Birckhead's faith and support have sustained me through the whole process.

And the vision to see in a teaching course and a work experience the possible seeds for a "basic" book rests with Matthew J. Culligan, an American business phenomenon in his own right. His collaboration and trust have been invaluable.

Kate Kelly shepherded the project through the labyrinths of publishing, and Robert Markel has lent his humor and dedicated support throughout the writing.

Books, unlike people, have more than two parents. I hope the many parents of this one take some pride in its creation and see it as a welcome addition to the library of business writing.

Mary Jean Parson
Teaneck, N.J.

To the hundreds of thousands of men and women in business and industry management who "keep the faith" and advance the cause of Humane Free Enterprise.

Matthew J. Culligan
New York, N.Y.

INTRODUCTION
"Why Back to Basics?"

What makes the difference between adequate individuals and organizations and great ones? The simple, one-word answer is *values.*

When considered in order of importance, the primary value is *philosophy.* What do individuals regard as their role in life? What is the basis of corporate missions?

Next on the list of values is *planning.* How do individuals realize their role in life? How do corporations realize their missions?

The purpose of this book is to get back to the basics of planning, for one of the harmful by-products of a long, continuous "bull market," such as we had in the United States after 1968, was the obfuscation of the basics. The introduction of computers and the mad rush to (sometimes ill-conceived) management information systems added to this departure from the basics. Also, overemphasis on the idea that an MBA degree is needed to understand management has, since the mid-1960s, contributed further to the movement of U.S. companies and entire industries away from the basics. Facts were often overshadowed by the techniques used to provide those facts.

Even during the ages when humans were hunter/gatherers, there was a need for planning. Indeed, survival itself depended on cooperation and planning. Later, when humans settled into agrarian societies—living in one locale with other clans and tribes and forced to store food and water and to keep records—the need for the planning became even more evident, and the planning process began. There soon came a time when things of value—food, clothing, weapons and tools—could no longer simply be traded on a one-to-one basis. It became necessary to devise symbols of those valuable items. This led to the development of a monetary system in which coins, metal ornaments and later diamonds and precious stones entered the human equation. This was part of the evolution of culture and civilization, and with it evolved basic planning.

The development of planning was accelerated enormously by the industrial revolution. There could have been no mass production without planning and effective transportation and communication. And now the United States is taking the first tentative steps into a new period, which might be termed the "scientific-planetary age." The planning that made possible the first manned space flight was mind-boggling to the average individual. We came to accept the old Chinese proverb "The longest journey begins with a single step." Not true! The longest journey actually begins with *thinking* about taking that first step—that is, with planning. Bluntly, our survival as a species may rest on good planning in this complex technological world.

Back-to-basics planning, such as we deal with in the course of this book, takes into account these present and prospective interrelationships.

Employing the principles of back-to-basics planning should assist you in becoming noticeably effective in your position. Superiority in planning is the best kind of visibility to have within an organization, for it is generally agreed that the only viable plan is a *written* plan, and written plans become part of the record.

Moreover, this book is geared for the so-called nonfinancial manager. Planning and management do not require an MBA, an accounting degree or a CPA certificate. They require tools, skills and an ability to take an overview of the venture's current and future.

In fact, as this book was being researched and written, the

once-glamorous computer industry has been in turmoil. Some of the greatest names in the field have failed to market computers in sufficient numbers and at high enough prices to be profitable. There is one notable exception, the International Business Machines Corporation (IBM).

One of your authors spent years as a manager at RCA, which competed with IBM in computers. RCA ultimately abandoned the computer field, taking a write-off of over $500 million, though the total losses were closer to twice that sum. A subsequent examination of that failure disclosed a basic flaw in planning: RCA was a huge corporation and was successful in other product lines. But the planning group decided to take on IBM across the board—that is, compete in all computer sizes. It would have done better to have opted for less than a full-line assault, carving out a niche for itself well within its capabilities.

The great General Electric Corporation likewise decided to compete with IBM across the board. It also failed, but in its planning, it provided for an exit with honor. GE sold its computer division to another corporation and avoided the embarrassment suffered by RCA.

A decade later yet another large corporation, Texas Instruments, entered the computer field and was initially successful. But its planners did not anticipate that IBM would enter the microcomputer field. When IBM did launch its Personal Computer line, Texas Instruments' sales plummeted. Texas Instruments wisely abandoned the computer field, and its stock took an upward leap, even though the company's losses probably totaled half a billion dollars or more.

What is IBM's secret? A study of IBM from the outside and discussions with former IBM executives have led to the conclusion that Thomas Watson, the genius who developed the corporation, and his contemporaries at IBM left a legacy of product planning—a legacy that can be summed up in the following formula:

Step 1. Logic (consensus that a new product is logical)
Step 2. Design
Step 3. Prototypes (as many as necessary)
Step 4. Manufacturing sample (cost-effective)
Step 5. Quality control
Step 6. Tactical marketing

The foregoing product-planning formula comes under the heading of strategic marketing. You apply the tenets of strategic planning as part of every back-to-basics planning exercise relating to new products and new services.

Good total planning is fundamental to every aspect of life, whether it be running a company, directing your own career or locating the right college for your child. The philosophy, the process, the techniques are the same. For that reason, this book should have a broad appeal, not only to those of you who wish to apply its principles in your business environment but to all of you who, in your personal lives, have enough pride and ambition to want to arm yourselves with the knowledge and precepts that can do your best in meeting any challenge you may face.

Back-to-basics planning is not a magic elixir. But it is a beacon of logic and direction in a rapidly changing world.

Mary Jean Parson
Matthew J. Culligan

1 THE PLANNING PHILOSOPHY

"It takes all the running you can do to keep in the same place. To get ahead, you must run twice as fast as that."
—Lewis Carroll, *Through the Looking Glass*

Running twice as fast is a technique used by failures. While successful companies and successful people do run as fast as they can, they also run in a predetermined direction—one that has been identified and analyzed. The secret, then, isn't to run twice as fast, but to run steadily on a carefully charted course. The secret is good planning.

Back-to-basics planning requires on outline. The outline keeps you on course, it takes away the mystery and tedium, and it eliminates error—because, quite simply, if you follow the outline you won't forget anything. But before the outline can be written, the planning philosophy must be considered.

VITAL ELEMENTS OF THE
BACK-TO-BASIC PLANNING PHILOSOPHY

But of Course I Know What My Business Is All About!

The *philosophy* of the firm itself is fundamental to back-to-basics planning. It encompasses the nature, the function, the objective of the operation in which you are involved. The need to formulate and adhere to this philosophy cannot be stressed enough. To put it succinctly, the philosophy of a business clarifies intentions and starts the process of identifying potential problems and solutions.

Are we profit or nonprofit? Self-serving, client-serving, stockholder-serving? Community-minded or organizationally minded? In short, what are we specifically in business to do? (Keep the word specific close to your heart. Ford Motor Company is not in business to make cars; it is in business to make money for its shareholders by making cars.) What should we do, and how should we do it? If your business philosophy is fuzzy, then no plan can be written that will make good business sense.

The philosophy of your company is basic. Of course you know what your business is all about! (Don't you?) Have you written it down lately?

Flexibility is also vital to good business planning. We must be able to adjust to a changing environment. The world is not the same as it was five minutes ago or five months ago, much less five years ago. "Business as usual" is almost surely doomed to failure. The plans that you write today could be out of date by the time you have them printed and distributed. That does not mean that it is useless to write plans but rather that they must be *organic* and *monitored* (words that you will read constantly in this book) based on your flexibility in a changing world. Technological advances, legal changes and societal developments will affect your plan and your venture's success. "Rolling with the punches" and "improvising" are defensive, not offensive, actions. A preplanned strategy of flexibility gives you the edge over the competition.

Personnel development is another area that takes on more significance in a rapidly changing environment. The currently unemployed steel workers, automobile workers and railroad workers who may never again find jobs in their former fields represent a truly difficult issue. The sad and depressing truth, which our politicians and business leaders skirt with trepidation, is out there for all to see. Technology, world trade, international politics, the educational system—all have left a substantial portion of the American work force reeling in the wake of a tidal wave of change.

The development of personnel (in terms of their education, skills and knowledge) is a two-pronged responsibility. Management cannot afford to allow its employees to fall behind the competition. Neither can an employee be complacent, resting on the comfort of a union contract or in the lap of a benign management and allowing the future to engulf him or her.

Organization planning (which we will discuss later) is basic to addressing the personnel-development issue. Some of the key questions in this area are:

How many people do you need?
What kind of people?
Do you hire them away from others or train them yourselves?
Do you create a mix of new blood and trained blood to build the vitality a healthy company needs?
Do you plan ahead or let it just "happen"?

Superior planning is the bedrock on which all sound business practices must be based. There is little room for luck in a highly competitive world. The plan is a road map to a goal. But it's not cast in stone. The plan isn't written to sit on a bookshelf, neatly printed and bound between stylishly embossed covers. Quite the contrary. It is an organic entity, like a plant. It grows and changes. And if nurtured and cared for in an orderly and regular way, the plan will flourish and bloom, just like the plant.

THE NEED FOR FORMALIZATION

Why must the plan be formalized? If you have a good idea, and you've got the backing and the timing is right, why can't you just "go for it"? The answer is simple: *time, technological change* and *complexity.*

"Time and tide wait for no man [or woman]." The pressures of time, the rising tide of technological changes and the increasing complexity of society create a business environment dangerous to the unwary and unprepared. Not so long ago, for example, a bad musical on Broadway could lose its backers $500,000 overnight. Now they can lose $4 million. That's a big impact, even in this economy.

The *time* needed to analyze the competition and the options has become crucial to business success. The time needed to make sound business decisions is *lengthening*, and the impact of poorly planned, quick business decisions has become enormous. We need time—not to worry and wonder, but to think and plan for the alternatives in a competitive world.

Technological change has speeded up so significantly and affected every business so completely that to launch a business venture without adequate knowledge both of what is and of what will be is almost foolhardy. It is safe to say that no career or business from these days forward will be untouched by technology in its many and rapidly changing forms.

The *complexity* of our environment—in terms of political, cultural, societal, demographic and legal changes—dictates that a wealth of specialized knowledge be applied to ensure the success of any venture. That may be the saddest comment. Challenges can be fun to a venturesome individual; but the need for specialists in our society appears to have taken away some of the fun. The need for the so-called Renaissance man or woman in this society may be diminishing; the generalist may have become an endangered species. However, it is our contention that those generalists will ultimately make the best managers, the best CEOs, the best visionaries because they can see the whole picture, pull it together, articulate it and emerge as the consummate planners of the future. Let's hear it for a liberal arts/humanities undergraduate education for the managers of the future! Their broad perspective of the world could give them the edge in these rapidly changing latter years of the twentieth century.

Ultimately, then, the orderly back-to-basics planning process allows the planner/manager to look at a problem/opportunity from a different perspective. A lawyer, an accountant, an engineer or a designer will inevitably look at the world from their particular perspective—not wrong, but specialized. Good planners examine many facets of the situation and see the venture differently. As illustrated in the story of the group of blind men feeling an elephant (each made a definitive pronouncement about the nature of the beast based on his own limited perspective), the person who is able to take a broad overview of an entire situation (the sighted person) has a far better chance of grasping the true nature of a problem/opportunity (the elephant) and acting upon that knowledge.

What you're really looking for, then, in good business planning is the opportunity for long-term growth. Every business venture should have a future (even a one-night television special is presumed to have subsidiary rights, preplanned). The formalized back-to-basics plan is the key to that growth.

THE BACK-TO-BASICS PLANNING PROCESS

It helps to think of the planning process as the classic pyramid. If planning begins at the management level (the point of the pyramid) and trickles down through the ranks (to the base), it is probably doomed to failure. You know what happens to a pyramid when it is stood up on its point: it falls over (Figure 1.1). Back-to-basics planning should begin at the base of the pyramid and work its way up through the organization—from the individual level to the departmental level to the divisional level to the corporate—because if it is built block by block from the ground up, the plan, like the pyramid, will be sound, strong and enduring (Figure 1.2).

Take a moment to think of a few people you consider to be good managers. What are some of the names? Is Lee Iacocca a good manager? How about Joe Papp? Ed Koch? Why do you say yes or no? What is your perception of their planning styles? Well, only their employees can tell us for sure what makes such managers tick, but we can make certain assumptions. During the planning process, a good manager undoubtedly trusts his or her subordinate managers, requests input from those managers and incorporates their ideas into the plan. It is doubtful that anyone regarded as a good planner/manager is an autocrat, imposing the elements of the plan from the top down on the departmental managers.

The plan itself, by the way, is not the most important thing in a business. The *process* of planning is the most important activity. If done properly, this process involves everyone in the venture. So what happens? Everyone has a vested interest in making the venture work! It's always more likely that a venture will succeed if everyone pulls the wagon in the same direction than if several go off down paths of their own choosing, leaving the wagon stuck in the middle of the road.

The last sort of attitude you want in a business is, "That's not my problem." Or, "That's not what I thought would happen." Or, "I didn't agree with that; why should I work for it?" A back-to-basics plan must therefore be total, it must be comprehensive, it must relate each aspect with all others, and it must involve everyone in its objectives and strategies. Any manager responsible for costs, services and revenues will do best when he or she is required to develop a back-to-basics plan.

"What Goes Up Must Come Down"

A good manager in the planning process always facilitates a continuing dialogue between departments and between all levels of management. Any plan that isolates departments and individuals from the overall process is a plan for disaster. Check the comparison between the planning process and the communications flow shown in Figure 1.3. As noted earlier, the planning process (represented in the figure by the dark arrows) moves upward through the blocks (the departments) in order for a viable plan to be developed. However, when we look at those same departmental blocks from a communications standpoint, the communications flow (represented by the light arrows) must move downward and laterally as well as upward. That is, people should be encouraged to communicate with their peers, their superiors and their subordinates.

Figure 1.1
The Precarious Pyramid, Which Teeters
on a Narrow Point of Top-Level Support

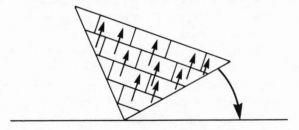

Figure 1.2
The Stable Pyramid, Which Rests
on a Wide, Solid Base of Ground-Level Support

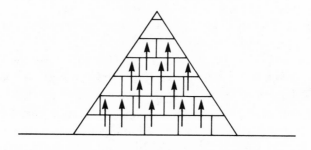

Figure 1.3
The Planning Process Compared to
the Communications Flow

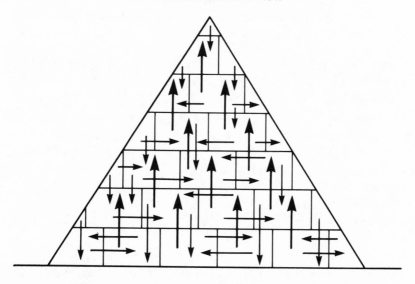

NOTE:= planning process; = communications flow.

QUALITATIVE AND QUANTITATIVE STANDARDS

All planning decisions take into account at least two kinds of
standards: qualitative and quantitative. Among the fundamental
qualitative standards in the business-planning field are:

- Management development. Who is in the slot? What if a truck hit the boss tomorrow? Must we go out and buy talent, or are we growing it here?
- Image. How do I want this company to be perceived? By the public? (Which public?) The stockholders? The employees? The government(s)?
- Contribution to the community. What do we owe to our community? What can we give to it? What will we get back?
- Talent development. What about our future? Who are our thinkers and creators? Is a competitor getting ahead of us?
- Technical advancement. What's going on that will affect us? Can we afford to wait? What are the risks? What are the advantages?
- Political/social influence. What is our balance with production partners? With trading partners? Does a government agency present looming problems? Should we take a stand? Should we be out in front, leading our industry toward new horizons?

Quantitative standards are those that ask the question, "How much?" These are the familiar names that often appear in financial statements:

Budgets	Customers	Assets
Costs	Share	Liabilities
Revenues	Profits	Profit margins
Volume	Losses	

PLANNING AS A PROCESS OF STRUCTURED CREATIVITY

The planning cycle is the greatest opportunity a business will have in getting its people to talk to each other, to share with each other, to work off each other. It is the opportune moment for people to come out of their departmental isolation and share their vision, their dreams, their problems, their ideas about the company and its future.

But if too many voices express themselves simultaneously, the effect becomes one of interference, just as when we yell, "I can't hear you when the water's running."

Obviously, you are not interested in creating a modern-day

Tower of Babel. Rather, there must be an orderly procedure delineating what people should be talking about. Weighing that input, putting it in perspective, working the trade-offs is the job of the executive in charge. But the process of sharing can be guided and focused by the format and requirements of the plan itself. Within its boundaries, a great deal of freewheeling creativity can have full rein.

One of us can remember with great delight the preliminary planning meetings held in Florida one summer week as director of planning for a leisure division of a major corporation. The general managers of two park attractions, the marketing managers of the two parks, the division controller, the division marketing director, the advertising agency representative and I locked ourselves in a room for three days, planning the five-year future of those attractions. Any idea, no matter how ridiculous, was written on the board the first day. By the third day, we had the outline for a plan; but more important, we had a consensus regarding the plan and how we would all work to make it effective. You never know where a good idea is going to come from, so structured creativity, within the back-to-basics planning framework, is one way to unlock an exciting future.

The buck must stop somewhere. And once the plans of departments and divisions are articulated, executive decision making takes over. The final decisions will be made in light of the overall needs of the company, which we will discuss later. But a fundamental back-to-basics planning principle is cooperative activity.

ORDERLY MONITORING OF THE PLAN

All of this structured creativity is useless unless there is a formalized way to monitor the *progress* of the plan. Summary reports, performance data, revised estimates, reaffirmations, updates—all must become a part of the ongoing life not only of the plan but of the business itself. In a later chapter, we deal with the use of *action plans* to direct and monitor the implementation of the back-to-basics plan.

THE ROLE OF MANAGEMENT IN THE PLANNING PROCESS

Good management, when most successful, is like two sides of a coin: It must combine *fiscal responsibility* and *integrity* with *creativity* and *vision*. Just as it is impossible to separate the two sides of a coin, so it is impossible to separate these elements of good management. We could all play the game of "guess the company" and try to name outstanding firms that combine these elements. If you name a company that you perceive as satisfying the above criteria, chances are you will have named a company that is also a success in the American and/or world marketplace. The formula, quite frankly, works.

And what is the role of executive management in the back-to-basics planning process? We hinted at it earlier, but we can be more specific:

Balance the requests and goals of the various departmental and divisional plans. This is where an in-depth understanding and a comprehensive interpretation of the qualitative and quantitative standards become absolute necessities in making the final choices.

Review and give realistic appraisals. Feed back. If a plan goes up the line and never comes back for review, evaluation, commendation, modification, implementation, it is useless. Remember the arrows going both ways on the pyramid! People can't join the team if they don't know what the overall corporate goals are.

Resolve conflicts and trade-offs. This is why they pay presidents so much. They make the hard decisions. Does that division get a new manufacturing plant, or do we allocate the money to another division for research? Do we add more personnel in that department, or do we increase the advertising budget that quarter instead? The charge has been leveled in recent years that "fast-track" chief executives, who join a company with the intent of staying only a few years, make trade-off and expenditure decisions based on short-term profits (and benefits for themselves) instead of long-term growth for the company. In some instances the charges may be justified; but remember our criteria for good management, and pattern yourself after the best. Keep those standards in mind, and evaluate the conflicts you face in light of them.

Be the final arbiter of profits, growth, image. How many of you have prepared a plan/budget and had it sent back to you with the terse directive, "Cut 10 percent of your costs"? That approach is short and effective; but as a manager, you'd like to know why. Executive management must weigh current profits against long-term development and weigh both against the firm's public image. And then top-level managers should share the reasons for those decisions with the subordinate managers involved. Remember the team.

Be an effective presenter of the company's goals to its many publics. The real test is during a crunch. We are reminded of the oil crisis in 1973 and the subsequent media laceration of oil company profits. Some oil companies came out as villains, some as tough, honest fighters. Think about it; weren't your perceptions of the difference formed by the way various companies spoke to you, the public? The *presentation* of the company—to the employees, the stockholders, the general public, the government(s)—is the most challenging job of any chief executive, because in a free-enterprise society, public opinion is as important as hard fact on a balance sheet. Caesar's wife was never more challenged than an American CEO, because not only must the company be honest, it must also be *perceived* to be honest.

In summary: What are the most valuable assets executive management can marshall in this highly competitive world? *Honesty, integrity and credibility* are worth their weight in gold. In the long run these traits win out over all others. The back-to-basics planning process, when done in an orderly, open, cooperative manner, paves the way for that kind of management and that kind of business practice.

Thus, planning is a generic function of management. It is not outside the mainstream of business; it is a fundamental, organic part of the day-to-day operation. There is no such thing as managers and planners and workers. There are only employees of a company or venture—all of whom *plan* the way they're going to run their part of the business. That's basic.

BACK-TO-BASICS PLANNING TOOLS

"For lack of a nail, the shoe was lost; for lack of a shoe, the horse was lost; for lack of a horse..." Well, the Battle of Waterloo might have been lost that way. But there is no reason for *you* to lose out due to lack of the proper fundamental planning tools.

There is no mystery about the back-to-basics planning process. The development and use of a few simple tools allow the manager or executive to do what businesspeople do best—to *think* and to *act*. Those tools, and the planning process, can help free management and staff from needless improvisation and error.

The rest of this book will be devoted to removing the mystery and getting back to the basics of sound, generic planning. The topics to be covered are as follows:

- Chapter 2 provides an overview of the *planning process*, including a discussion of each of the major components of a back-to-basics plan.

- Chapter 3 provides an *outline for the back-to-basics plan*. It consists of a series of forms corresponding to each major section of the plan. These provide the back-to-basics planner with a readily adaptable format for presenting all the information that should be contained in an effective business plan.

- Chapter 4 discusses the development and implementation of *strategic plans*, including the major strategic areas of concern to the planner.

- Chapter 5 traces the development of the back-to-basics *marketing plan*, from consideration of the initial concept through advertising and launching the product. Marketing tactics and philosophy are considered, and a series of forms is presented to serve as tools for creating the marketing plan.

- Chapter 6 discusses the use of management by objectives to develop an effective *organization plan* that will ensure that the venture's overall business effort is supported by the right people at the right time. Included are sections covering obstacles that the back-to-basics organization planner may encounter and strategies for overcoming them.

- Chapter 7, on *financial reports*, not only presents examples of forms to be used but discusses the philosophy underlying the use of such forms as tools for establishing financial control.

- Chapter 8 discusses the characteristics of the planner—the qualities and abilities that distinguish the back-to-basics planner and ensure his or her success within the organization.

CHECKLIST FOR THE PLANNING PHILOSOPHY

"The longest journey begins with [thinking about taking] a single step."

With apologies to Lao Tzu, the above quote is a reminder for the journey you will begin: planning the future—of your department, your venture, your life.

The planning philosophy is no more and no less basic than brushing your teeth every morning and evening. For the planning philosophy, which starts as a conscious thought process, can evolve into a habit that soon becomes second nature to the back-to-basics planner. A careful review of the following fundamental principles of the back-to-basics planning philosophy can help you form your own ingrained planning habit:

- Identify sound business practices for your venture.
- Determine your company's philosophy; simply stated, what is our nature and function?
- Remain flexible in a changing environment.
- Personnel development and training are crucial activities. Implement an ongoing program to ensure the growth of your people.
- Formalize the planning process, remembering that it is organic and must be monitored.
- Don't lose sight of your objective: You are planning for long-term growth.
- Good planning is like a pyramid, built from the bottom up, block by block.
- People have a vested interest in the success of a plan if they participate in the planning process.
- A successful plan must be total, comprehensive, relate each aspect with all others and involve everyone in formulating its objectives and strategies.
- Provide open and continuing dialogue between all departments and all levels of management. Don't isolate people.
- Develop qualitative and quantitative standards for your venture that are understood companywide.
- Since "you never know where a good idea will come from," you must devise a planning process that encourages

creativity at all levels.

- The proven traits of good management are fiscal responsibility and integrity combined with creativity and vision.
- Good management balances the requests and goals of the departments in light of these companywide qualitative and quantitative standards.
- Good management reviews and gives realistic appraisals and feedback.
- Good management resolves conflicts and trade-offs.
- Good management is the final arbiter of profits, growth, image. The buck stops somewhere.
- Planning is a generic function of management; it is an organic part of the day-to-day operation.
- Good planning tools free the firm's management and staff from needless improvisation and error.

2 THE PLANNING PROCESS

"There are nine and sixty ways of constructing tribal lays, and every single one of them is right."
—Rudyard Kipling, "In the Neolithic Age"

There is *no* universally correct way to write a plan. Each back-to-basics planner has his or her own favorite outline for implementing the planning *process*, and each recognizes that the process of writing the plan is what is fundamental. But the back-to-basics planner also knows that the uniformity of any plan's format makes the planning process easier for all concerned, both writer and reviewer/analyst. Thus, we offer the back-to-basics definitions and format for your business plan, culled from years of use in a variety of companies.

If you have ever found yourself in a foreign country where you do not speak the language, you are inevitably drawn to someone in a shop or restaurant who speaks *your* language. Although you may only exchange brief platitudes, you talk with the person because he or she understands you. Makes sense, doesn't it? Common words, common definitions—an agreement on the meaning of terms and phrases—make communication more comfortable, more rapid and more efficient.

The same is true in the planning process. If all concerned have a common agreement and a common understanding regarding the meaning of the words, the phrases and the requirements, then they communicate and work together better. Therefore, the *teaching* of the company's planning philosophy and its definition of terms is the necessary first step in making the process a meaningful experience to all.

In the present chapter, we will examine and define the elements of an effective back-to-basics plan. Defining these elements is the necessary first step in making the planning process a meaningful experience for everyone. (You may, of course, wish to modify these definitions according to the unique requirements of your own venture and the degree of detail that is needed.)

Once we have arrived at a shared understanding of the plan's elements (once we are all "speaking the same language," that is), Chapter 7 will present a series of forms that serve as an outline, or format, for implementing the back-to-basics planning process. They enable the back-to-basics planner to effectively summarize and present the information represented by each element of the plan.

ASSUMPTIONS

In an orderly planning process, a planning packet is given to each manager in order that the finished products will follow the same formats and therefore, be easy to review and to consolidate. Uniformity of the packet in no way inhibits the creativity and individuality of each planner/manager.

The first page of that packet, typically, contains the *economic assumptions* which the management has made regarding the coming planning period. (See Chapter 7, Figure 7.1.)

These are the guidelines which each planner/manager should follow when preparing the plan, and they concern such basics as salary increases, expected rent increases (or decreases), expected inflation rates, industry trends on pricing, cost of goods, etc.

This page helps each planner/manager *speak from a common base* in the preparation of the plan. It should also allow the preparer to identify *individual assumptions* which may vary from national trends (such as regional rent differences, changing regional telephone rates, salary competition, etc.)

PROJECT

The "project" portion of the plan (see Chapter 7, Figure 7.2) can range in scope from defining an entire company to defining a single department. It can be a simple statement, a paragraph of 5 lines or an essay of 5 to 10 pages. It answers two questions:

Mission—what the venture *is.*

Function—what the venture *does.*

A new Company has a mission: It is a privately owned computer company targeted to the home computer market. Its function is to develop, test, manufacture, market and distribute computers for the home computer market both in the United States and abroad. The definitions in each case could be more elaborate, but when the company was first conceived in the mind of an aggressive entrepreneur, those bare-bones definitions could have served as the introduction to the plan.

The personnel department of New York-based XYZ Corporation has a mission: It serves the employee-relations needs of all divisions of the corporation throughout the United States. Its function is to formulate and implement personnel policies and procedures, process all personnel transactions, monitor and process all benefits programs, coordinate organizational reviews and salary administration, and advise and consult with managers on personnel matters.

Keep in mind that the back-to-basics approach uses simple, declarative sentences in the "Project" portion of the plan. It should not tell too little, but neither should it tell too much. (In plans covering multimillion-dollar ventures, we have seen splendid project definitions that acquit themselves admirably in one succinct sentence.)

OVERVIEW

The "overview" portion of the plan (see Chapter 7, Figure 7.3) places your venture in perspective. It concerns itself with the *environment* (the world in which your venture operates), *business* (the field in which your venture competes) and the *future* (your hard-nosed, no-nonsense analysis of what lies out there as threat or opportunity).

Environment

The "Environment" portion of the "Overview" addresses itself to the old vaudeville gag line, "Everybody has to be somewhere." Where are you? More important, are you in the right place? You'll only know when you research and analyze the aspects of the environment listed below. Again, brevity is not necessarily a virtue, but clarity and honesty are. If you are running a theater, your "environment" could be the SMSA (Standard Metropolitan Statistical Area). If you're selling computers, it could be the whole world. Therefore, of necessity, the following definitions are broad generalities. The specifics will depend on the nature of your particular venture.

- *Economic.* What is the state of the economy now, and what is it expected to be in the coming year? How will this impact on your venture? We suggest that certain economic assumptions be arrived at on the corporate level so that everyone is making the same assumption. (No need for one person to anticipate an inflation rate of 10 percent and another to assume 5 percent.) The Conference Board, Chase Econometrics and other resources help take the mystery out of these assumptions; they may not be right, but decisions will at least be based on uniform assumptions, allowing for an easier adjustment of the whole plan in the future.
- *Cultural/social.* What is going on in terms of changing lifestyles that could impact on your plan? If you manufacture hot tubs, the regional trends can be significant; they certainly are in the creation of television programming and the printing of Spanish textbooks. You ignore the cultural

shifts (not fads!) in this country, and others, at your peril.

- *Political.* These winds shift more often than the Gulf Stream, but knowledge of changing laws and regulations, the power to influence them and the growth or diminution of political groups can have a profound effect on the thrust of a business plan. Keep informed—not only of those matters that interest you but also of those that don't.

- *Demographic.* This word, which has taken its place in the American language over the past two decades, predominantly involves statistical data that describe who we are. The sophistication of data collection has reached an amazing state these days, as all of us know who pull direct-mail solicitations out of our mailboxes. "Sample precincts" have been analyzed to such a degree that elections can now be predicted with less than 2 percent of the vote. Each of us is categorized at least by age, sex, race, income, political registration, marital status, reading habits, television and radio habits (including cable), purchases of necessities and luxury items, travel habits and religion. There are many more elements in computers around the country (including those of the IRS), and the bulk of this information is available to marketers and to planners for use in the preparation of their plans. The Commerce Department, the Department of Labor and *Advertising/Marketing* magazine are good resources, as are the Conference Board and other individual research firms.

- *Technological.* Analysis of and preparation for the technology of the present as well as the future with respect to your venture is a crucial part of your business planning. This can range from an analysis of a new telephone system (now that you have a lot of choices), to satellite transfer of data or funds, to the use of word processors in the efficient storage and reproduction of data, to the development of new chemical processes to alter organic and mineral elements. Remember, the future is now. Keep up with it!

- *Artistic/development.* What are your plans to nurture the creative mind? You think you don't need creativity? Wrong! The creative writers, the scientists, the researchers, the developers, the artists, the musicians, the thinkers in your organization can be worth their weight in gold. Have you planned for their recruitment, their training, their comfort, their enthusiasm, their technical and creative needs? These aren't silly questions. Everything we wear, use, eat, drink and, frankly, think was created by somebody; and creative artists are happy starving only in operas such as *La Bohème* More seriously and to the point, the 3-M Company (Minnesota Mining and Manufacturing) is the classic example of a company rich in products, prestige and profitability (will the "three p's" replace the "three r's"?) because its creative development people are allowed a great deal of freedom, flexibility and leeway to "team." That's how 3-M gets new products, employee loyalty and a reputation for excellence. How comfortable are creative people in *your* environment?

- *Internal.* This is the section in which you look candidly at your current internal environment. This can mean everything from the amount of space you occupy and the ambience of your company's/department's surroundings (don't be fooled; cramped quarters, dingy surroundings and a rotten neighborhood can affect employee interest and productivity) to the attitudes and relationships of the people working together (if the boss's son is your boss, be careful; but if political intrigue is taking more time than business calls, then address the problem—obliquely and with euphemisms, probably, but address it).

Business

As a continuing part of the "Overview," you will now look at your business as it relates to other companies in the same field.

- *Critical success factors.* What is *critical* to your success next year? If you're in sales and you're waiting for a new product to be tested and hit the market, it's pretty critical that the rollout timetable be adhered to in order for you to make your target. If your increase in productivity is tied to a new piece of equipment, it's critical that you be given the capital funds to purchase that equipment. If you plan to open up a territory of a new office in order to increase sales or compete with another company, it is crucial that you get the money for the facility and the additional personnel.

- *Competitive position.* Don't try to "fool the foolers." Don't be aggressively optimistic about how great your company or division is compared with its competition; management knows about as much as you do in this area. Be honest and succinct. This is where statistics come in handy. Here you can compare size of staff, share of market, gross revenues, productivity of employees—any number of factors that define your position with respect to the competition.
- *Trends/industry developments.* This is where your constant, year-round reading of trade journals pays off. Of course you keep a folder in your desk drawer into which you drop interesting clippings all year, so that when it comes to writing this section, you are up to date on major industry trends. You will also avail yourself of the industry organization to which your company belongs to obtain information on statistics and specific trends. And you will footnote your sources to avoid needless questions.
- *Strengths.* Honestly and candidly, what are the strong points of your division or company? Do you have the best training program in the business (turning out lower-cost aggressive tigers)? Do you have solid professionals across all or most of your departments? Do you enjoy a good reputation with your customers/clients? (Can a survey prove it?) Does your company lead in the production of new, exciting products? Is your theater sold out? Do you have the highest ratings in your time slot?
- *Weaknesses.* Shortcomings, too, should be addressed honestly and candidly. It is no sin for a manager to admit a weakness in his/her department or company (it could be regarded as a glaring oversight not to recognize it). This is the place in the plan to identify internal problems. Later in the plan you will have the opportunity to develop strategies to solve them.

Future

The "Future" section of the plan is not the place to dream (that comes later, in your long-range plan). This is the place to address specific problems and opportunities you see down the years for your segment of the business.

- *Major Opportunities.* Are new laws or government regulations coming soon that will open up possibilities for increased business? Can you do business differently? (Could you, for example, pay your insurance premiums differently to improve your cash flow, reestablish your payroll period to improve your cash position or hire part-time employees for certain tasks?) Is your competition having trouble, thereby allowing you to step in? Is a major executive leaving a competing company, causing some dislocation in its mode of operation? And so on.
- *Major threats.* Go through the same sort of exercise that you did above; only this time identify problems that could limit future growth. Always remember, *some* problems can't be solved. When the FCC removed cigarette advertising from television, hundreds of millions of dollars in sales vanished with it. What to do? Developing new clients for network television was the answer, and retail sales were the target. In the final analysis, the money was barely missed, thanks to the implementation of an aggressive alternate plan. You will develop strategies to combat these threats in your alternate plans.

OPERATION PLAN

Now you get to the fun stuff. The "operating plan" (see Chapter 7, Figure 7.4) is where you identify *what* you want to do and *how* you want to do it.

Objectives

Objectives are generally one-sentence, *specific* statements of what the company, division or department wishes to accomplish. Some examples are:

Increase gross revenues 15 percent.
Increase profits 10 percent.
Enhance image with state............agency.
Increase audience reach by 3 percent.
Expand financial reports to include............division.

Implement salary administration system.

Develop and implement national advertising campaign for product.

It is unlikely that any division or department would have only *one* objective for the coming year (although nothing is impossible—Lee Iacocca could have established as his sole objective in 1979 "prevent bankruptcy" and then have devised many strategies for doing so). However, it is also atypical to assume that as many as 15 or 20 objectives could be accomplished in a number of *specific* objectives that it is reasonable for your particular venture to attempt to achieve.

Remember, be specific, be succinct and don't confuse *what* you want to do with *how* you want to do it.

Strategies

The "Strategies" section of the plan is your chance to say *how*. This is the place where all the homework you did in the "Overview" section of the plan begins to pay off. Coupled with your knowledge and imagination, that research will point the way toward the strategies you will implement. For instance, if your objective is to increase gross revenues by 15 percent, you may have 15 or 20 strategies for doing so. You could increase your advertising budget and also target some of it to a different market. You could open a new office or add sales personnel. You could introduce a new product or expand your theatrical repertory season or sell merchandising rights to a current product. As you can see, these are the *how's* of your plan.

In each case they must be logical and practical. In each case they may also impact on your operating budget, your capital requests, your personnel (and space/equipment) requests and your marketing budget. Therefore, you should be able to prove that they are worth the cost or that they will provide an adequate ROI (return on investment). That justification should rightly be included in your financial back-up statements (see Chapters 6 and 7).

Critical Factors

What happens if something goes wrong and you can't implement the plan? Remember the work you did in "Critical Success Factors," "Major Threats" and "Weaknesses"? What if you can't solve those problems? What if the corporation, for sound reasons involving the good of the overall company, can't comply with all your requests for capital or increased operating budget or extra personnel? What if the competition gets the jump on you and you didn't anticipate it? What if a government agency does pass that negatively impacting regulation?

This is the section where you make a list of those items that can go wrong with the plan (over which you, personally, have no control) and what the impact will be. A couple of examples are:

Capital budget for new office not granted:
 reduce revenues $1,500,000
 reduce expenditures $700,000
Sales personnel not added
 reduce revenues $ 800,000
 reduce expenses $ 500,000

Itemize the events and their impact. As you will see in Chapter 7 (Figure 7.7), each of the new projects and new activities is to be detailed anyway; this "Critical Factors" section allows you to measure the impact of each and enables the reviewer/analyst to rapidly develop a revised plan if the anticipated event does not occur.

Bear in mind that this section answers the question, "What is the impact if such an event occurs?" It does not answer the question, "What are you going to do about it?" That comes in the "Alternate Plans" section.

PLAN SUMMARY

This page (see Chapter 7. Figure 7.5) allows the planner/manager to give a quick overview of the financial expectations for the planning period. Obviously, it is to be used by departments or divisions which are responsible for revenues and profits. It is not to be used by service department heads who control only costs.

This example assumes a fiscal year which is the same as a calendar year. You can adapt it to your own fiscal reporting periods.

This is a page for management's benefit. It gives them a quick overview of your expectations in the planning period and also allows the reviewer to make a quick consolidation of all plans so that management can take a first look at the total picture.

It sets up the summary by quarter and year, as well as a summary of the first three months, three quarters and a year of your plan. The "detail" should be broad categories (see Figure 7.7 for examples).

DEPARTMENTAL OPERATIONS: NARRATIVE

The "Departmental Operations: Narrative" section of the plan (see Chapter 7, Figure 7.6) is your chance to write about your operation, to express your ideas, your philosophy, your vision. (Be careful! Some executives may not want too much philosophy.) But if you can express yourself in simple declarative sentences, this is a chance to illuminate your operation to management. Discuss next year's operations, as you have planned them, with a view toward how they will impact on your objectives and strategies. Pay particular attention to staffing, space requirements, equipment needs, work loads, and service and supply requirements. Talk about your staff; consolidate their ideas into the narrative. (They had a planning meeting with you, remember?) Discuss any ideas you have to streamline or improve operations, particularly if you have included them in your objectives and strategies. Can you reduce service requirements? Cut down on overtime? Boost productivity? Do you have ideas that might impact on other departments? Can you initiate further cooperation with others?

We have seen one-page narratives that are useless and one-page narratives that can change a company's concept of itself. Don't be embarrassed to get a good writer to help you. The idea is to represent the department or division well, not to take false pride in bad writing. Planning is a team effort anyway—so use the team!

If done well, the "Departmental Operations: Narrative" section of the plan can raise your work above the crowd and make you more visible to management.

NEW PROJECTS

Detailing new projects (see Chapter 7, Figure 7.7) helps clarify your thinking as you develop new strategies and undertakings to make your venture more profitable, more efficient, more visible and more productive. It compels you to put a cost alongside each strategy or project so you can, with clarity, analyze its worth (ROI).

Sometimes a department head will request new personnel simply to keep from drowning. Your "Departmental Operations: Narrative" is the chance to address this sort of justification when cold, hard dollars don't fill the bill. Remember, in many instances, having an ongoing personnel-turnover problem can be much more costly than hiring additional personnel to handle the work load in the first place. New equipment may also be needed to handle the work load; but that can be justified on the grounds of increased productivity, responding to growing company needs.

Most new-project requests have costs attached to them, but they don't always have to turn a profit. That's why the section "Objectives of New Project(s)" (on Figure 7.7) is so important. To facilitate its decision making, management needs to know *your* rationale. If you present a good case, management's response is likely to be positive.

If you use a separate page for *each* new-project request, it makes analysis and decision making easier. It also facilitates revision of the plan and budgets. This isn't "make-work." It speeds up handling of these essential documents at later stages in the planning process.

ALTERNATE PLANS

The "Alternate Plans" section is the one that answers the question, "What do I do if those things go wrong?" In Chapter 7 (Figure 7.8), we suggest that this information be presented in two parts: (1) "Narrative" and (2) "Financial Impact." The "Narrative" section allows you to elaborate on the actions you will take in case some of the events occur. The "Financial Impact" section allows you to measure the impact (on income, costs, profits) in an orderly way.

In our experience this becomes an exercise almost akin to selecting from a Chinese menu: "one from column A, two from column B." Management has gone through its trade-off process, as discussed in Chapter 1, and you have the go-ahead for some of your new strategies and a negative decision on others. You can put in those *accepted* items from your "New Projects" pages, remove items that have been *rejected* (again using the "New Projects" pages) and have a clear picture of your approved plan for the coming year.

We also include one other "Alternate Plans" page, which we suggest that you submit to management at the beginning (Chapter 7, Figure 7.9). Some managements have the opinion that all first plans have "fat" in them; they assume (rightly or wrongly) that you have embellished your requests in order to "give management something to cut." That may not be accurate, but if you know your company, you know how to play the game. This is not to say that we encourage the game; on the contrary, the best plan writing in our opinion is based on honest, realistic requests and goals. But on the assumption that every company arrives at hard times sometime, and that all managers have to "tighten their belts" for the good of the company on occasion, we suggest using the "Alternate Plans" form shown in Figure 7.9. Management can chop up your budget request like a woodcutter (with an ax), or it can allow you to trim your budget like a surgeon (carefully and selectively, so the patient will live). We believe the latter method is best, simply because it allows managers to manage. If you use that form, you will have identified both *what* you can cut and what the *impact* of those cuts will be (the obvious conclusion being that management must be willing to accept the impact if it requires the cuts).

Remember, the whole purpose of companywide back-to-basics business planning is not to develop a method of hiding something from top management; it is a way of sharing all ideas and information so that everyone may work together for the overall benefit of the enterprise and its employees.

ACTION PLANS

Action plans are not necessarily included in the plan package that is presented to management, but they are the *core* of your activity as a manager who is managing a department, a division or a venture. We present a simplified form in Chapter 7, Figure 7.10.

Action plans answer such questions as: Who is going to do it? When is it due? How much will it cost? They are the tool you use to *monitor* your plan.

The simplest way to approach an action plan is to go back to the "Strategies" section of your "Operating Plan." Every strategy becomes an action that must be accomplished. *Every* strategy should therefore be written down and responsibility, due date and budget assigned to it. Obviously, this is not an exercise performed by the manager in the privacy of his or her office, away from the staff who will implement the action plan. Since all your department heads have participated in the planning process, all the goals and strategies are a part of their plans anyway. *Together*, you should write up action plans for each strategy, sign off on the budgets, assign responsibility, agree on the completion dates and put the projects in motion.

These action plans can serve as status reports, which your subordinates will file with you on a regular basis (it can be once a week, every two weeks, once a month, once a year, but it must be *agreed* to). We have found that a status report every two weeks (assuming you have staff meetings or direct reports from your subordinates on alternate weeks) is adequate reporting to keep you informed of progress and problems and to allow your staff the necessary breathing room to accomplish its goals. Some people believe this is too often, but in the volatile world of American business, a lot can happen weekly and biweekly. While the last thing you want to do is hover over your staff, not knowing what's going on can lead to disaster.

The timing of the action plan status reports is *yours* to choose, but a decision to *forgo* monitoring the progress of the plan is simply foolhardy. The most satisfying word on a status report is *completed* over in the right-hand column. As you establish your plan and implement it, be sure that you monitor it and see it to completion.

FINANCIAL HISTORY

Figure 7.11 in Chapter 7 presents a suggested thumbnail "Financial History" sketch of the progress and opportunity of your venture. There are many variations on the theme, but a one-page summary such as this provides you and management with an overview that can identify meaningful trends. If you operate a department rather than a profit center, the form can be modified to include *categories* of costs, both controllable and noncontrollable. While a great deal of financial information is required in the planning process, the written narrative of the plan may be accompanied only by those details that illuminate, clarify and project future trends.

RESOURCE REQUIREMENTS

Resource requirements are sometimes called capital requests. We include a sample in Chapter 7 (Figure 7.12), but they will vary with the requirements of your own particular venture. The sample we present is based on the requirements of a corporation with a number of divisions. The capital requirements come from the corporate coffers—trade-offs are fundamental in this exercise. Sometimes, in addition to the capital required, corporations will charge the division or unit the current interest rate the corporation itself is paying for loans (although these same corporations are often reluctant to credit the division or unit for tax credits or for interest earned on daily cash flow from profits). However, identifying your capital resource requirements is a fundamental management responsibility (even if it involves nothing more than an $1,100 IBM Selectric typewriter). Don't overlook it in your plan; if you don't ask for something, you may not get it.

In the not-for-profit world, the "resource development" section of the plan can consist of hundreds of pages. These plans are as complex as the marketing plan of any major corporation in the country. We are not giving them short shrift in this book. But such plans have been dealt with in many other publications and are an art unto themselves.

LONG-RANGE PLANS

Now to the future. How do you see it? What is the position of your department, your venture, your company in it? The "Narrative" portion of the "Long-Range Plans" section allows you to present your projections covering the next 3 to 5 to 10 years, depending on the nature of your company. (If you make cars, 10 years is a short period of time. If you make television programs, 3 years is a lot.) The "Detail" portion of the section on long-range planning invites sensible budgeting but aggressive ideas in your area of operation. While the long-range plan is not binding (remember, planning is an *organic* process), it allows company management to share your long-range vision of the firm's destiny. Again, the research you did in the "Overview" section of the plan will come into play here. This does not mean that you must repeat the ideas of the media and gurus, but it does mean that your projections should be based on what *is* as well as what you think might *be*.

We suggest a brief, annotated narrative, followed by some reasonable guesses as to produced revenues, costs, headcount, new projects and profits (Chapter 7, Figure 7.13). Though not binding, when consolidated with other plans, this allows top management to view its future through the eyes of its principal employees. If you believe that planning and progress of a venture are based on the people who make it run, then use the "Long-Range Plans" section to capture your most creative thoughts. In Chapter 1 we said, "You never know where a good idea will come from." You can get a lot of "off-the-wall" ideas in long-range plans, but just remember, going to the moon was an "off-the-wall" idea, once upon a time. For executive management, the long-range plans of each department and division have to be the most interesting planning element of all, because they give the ultimate indication as to whether or not your venture is going in a creative, profitable, productive direction and whether or not you have the right people working with you to take you there.

HEAD COUNT

Speaking of people, many companies and ventures expect a "head-count" page as part of the plan (see Chapter 7, Figure 7.14). Such a section serves little purpose if it is not related to dollars, income and profit. But it can be extremely useful if coupled with other numbers, such as square-footage analysis of space utilized (multiply the head-count number by 225 square feet to see whether you over- or underutilize office space for your personnel); if compared to your EEO report of women and minorities in the top four categories (executives, professionals, technical, sales) to see whether you are a leader or a laggard in equal opportunity; or if used to analyze your medical, pension or holiday/vacation benefits on a cost-per-employee basis to see whether you surpass or lag behind the national average. Taken alone, a head count is relatively useless. But employed by analysts in your company in conjunction with other key data, it can help define your position in the past, present and future in a variety of very important business categories.

CHECKLIST FOR THE PLANNING PROCESS
"Speak the same language."

The *process* of writing a business plan is more important to you and your staff than the written plan itself. Going through the cooperative, creative, analytical, structured process of looking at your venture and its future can make you a real "expert." Defining the elements of such a plan and agreeing at the outset on the data to be included help ensure that all involved are "speaking the same language"—the language of back-to-basics planning.

The following are reminders of how you get everyone involved in a common planning exercise and in working toward common goals.

- Having the plan in written form ensures that it will be taken seriously, while the process of writing the plan makes the plan meaningful.
- Be sure you know the general environment in which you operate—in terms of economic, cultural/social, political, demographic, technological, artistic/development and internal factors.
- Be sure you know the business environment in which you compete: your critical success factors, your competitive position, industry trends and developments and your strengths and weaknesses.
- Have a clear understanding of your future opportunities and threats.
- Be specific about the objectives for your venture and target between 5 and 15 achievable goals.
- Relate the strategies to the objectives, realizing that there can be several strategies for achieving one objective.
- Plan ahead for what can go wrong: identify the critical factors and devise alternate plans to cope with them.
- Use the "Departmental Operations: Narrative" section of the plan to illuminate your operation/department/division for management.

- Use the "New Projects" section to exhibit your ability to see into the future, to visualize, to relate to the company's long-term growth.

- Use the "Alternate Plans" section accurately and in great detail so that management will be more apt to let you manage your own operation rather than make decisions for you.

- In conjunction with your staff, develop action plans for all the strategies and set up a regular monitoring and review timetable.

- Be sure that your resource requirements (capital requests) include everything you may need in the coming period. If you don't ask for something, you may not get it.

- In long-range planning, present sensible budgets, but be sure they are coupled with aggressive ideas.

- Your "Head-count" page is a good tool for measuring your enterprise against the competition—in terms of space utilization, benefits, EEO, etc.

3 THE STRATEGIC PLAN

"*Strategy: the science and art of employing the armed strength of a belligerent to secure the objects of a war, especially the large-scale planning and directing of operations in adjustment to combat area, possible enemy action, political alignments...*"

—Webster's New Collegiate Dictionary

During the mid-twentieth century, the word strategy has come into common usage in the business world and is in fact the key process through which major businesses dominate their markets. Despite the different context in which the word is presently employed, the object of strategy is still the same—to win.

Until recently, all companies were structured in a hierarchy directly derived from the military (more about that in Chapter 5, which discusses the organization plan). Strategic planning, though, is as fundamental to the long life of a business venture as it is to a country. Thus, what must be regarded as the key words from Webster are: *the large-scale planning and directing of operations.*

SEVEN MAJOR STRATEGIC AREAS

Large-scale planning is fundamental to the success of any company. And the major strategies that give a firm its direction fall into seven areas. Success lies in *all* of these areas, not just a select few.

New or changed products? A business exists to furnish products or services. The profits that result mean many things to many people, but mostly, they are a very important measure of how well an enterprise serves its customers.

The fundamental questions are: Do we serve our customers well? Are changes needed in our product(s)? Are we lagging behind competition? Does a need exist that we are eminently qualified to satisfy? If so, should we develop a product/service to meet that need?

Marketing. Remember the words of Nietzsche: "The greatest stupidity is to lose sight of what one is trying to do." Marketing strategies are designed to guide the planning process in getting a product or service to a user. All else is frill.

Growth. Growth strategies are the company's answer to such questions as: How much growth? How fast? How soon? Must we preserve capital or invest it? Are we prepared to serve our customers if we spark growth now? (The nightmare of any planner must be to get the public interested in buying a product, only to have them find that it is not yet on the shelf—for whatever reason: shortage of raw materials, inadequate delivery systems, lack of sufficient personnel, etc.) They say bigger is better. But is that true in your own venture's particular situation?

Financial. Every business must have a clear strategy for financing its operations. Depending only on profits produced, hoping the banks will refinance a loser, trusting that advertising and public relations will salvage a damaged product/service reputation and all the other errors we read of daily can never take the place of sound financial planning, both for the present and for the foreseeable future.

Organizational. What type of organization is best for your business? The classic pyramid hierarchy may be right for one firm, while the "quality circle" may be better for another. (Apple Computers is not structured like IBM, but they both make pretty good computers.) How centralized should the firm be? What kinds of departmental structures and interfacing are required? What positions and job ladders are most suitable? Are the divisions responsible for profits? How should staffs be designed, recruited, trained and organized?

Personnel. Major strategies in the area of human resources give direction to the composition of the enterprise itself. They vary widely and involve such issues as unions, compensation, selection, recruitment, training and appraisal. The bottom line is: What kind of people do we want to be?

Public relations/advertising. These functions are not independent from the main business but rather must support all other major strategies. They are designed to illuminate a company's business to a variety of publics: customers, government(s), shareholders, suppliers.

DEVELOPING MAJOR STRATEGIES

In developing major strategies of any kind, you should perform a corporate self-appraisal, analyze the consistency of your strategies and develop strategies to meet unforeseen contingencies.

Corporate self-appraisal. What is our business? It is surprising how many companies don't really know what they are. The classic case is, of course, the railroads in America, which for too long overlooked the fact that they were in the *transportation* business, not in railroading. And as we know, bye-bye railroads. Glass bottles are really containers for liquid. In the go-go 1960s, when mergers were the quickest way to an improved balance sheet and a higher stock price, many companies got into businesses they knew nothing about and in which they had no experience and, in many cases, no real interest. While "conglomerates" may be here to stay, the evidence suggests that mergers are now based on some kind of business synergism rather than only on achieving a larger balance sheet or boosting short-term profits.

Assuring consistency of strategies. We have touched on this in Chapter 1, but it is well worth reemphasizing. Establishing consistency between departments, between divisions, between companies, striving for a common goal is the hardest task in appraising plans. Remember, in the Introduction, the example of RCA and IBM. In launching a totally new manufacturing division (computers), RCA may have made a classic error in taking on IBM across the board, in all sizes. If the object of a conglomerate is to make all divisions profitable, then consistency would have dictated carving out a share of the computer marketplace and building on that success. Other similar examples will cross your path every day. Never lose sight of the word *consistency*.

Developing contingency strategies. What do you do when things go wrong? After the plan has been written and evaluated, and after it has been adjudged both sound (in light of your corporate self-appraisal) and consistent, *then* what do you do if the world (either internal or external) changes under your feet? We have heard planning described as the process you go through to take care of the "known" so that you'll have time to take care of the unexpected when it occurs. (And it will!) *Reappraisal, monitoring* and *reviewing* on a regular basis are a must for management to ensure that the contingency strategies are continually updated.

RULES FOR IMPLEMENTING STRATEGIES

And finally, in implementing strategies, some cardinal rules must be followed:

- Strategies should be communicated to *all* key decision-making managers. Remember the pyramid: That which goes up should come down. We assume that the subordinate managers were part of the analysis and planning process; now they should know the results and the company's goals.
- All premises (assumptions) critical to the planning process must be developed and *communicated* to all managers. What is our collective view of the environment in which we will be functioning?
- *Action plans* must contribute to and impact upon major objectives and strategies. These are tactical programs for getting it done. Who, when, how, for how much?
- Strategies should be *reviewed* regularly. Monitor, monitor, monitor. Status reports are crucial.
- Develop *contingency plans* for all objectives and strategies.
- Make your *organization* fit your plans. It must be designed to support the accomplishment of goals. The refrain "This is the way we've always done it" should be banned from your premises. While wholesale housecleaning is not a planning

device (although the nonproductivity of white-collar workers *is* becoming a very lively topic in the popular press), the proper allocation of human resources to those areas in which they can perform best is not a hit-or-miss proposition. It is a fundamental process in accomplishing goals.

■ Continue to *teach* planning and strategy implementation in your organization. Lip service to planning by chief executives is a surefire guarantee of its failure. When the person at the top *believes* in back-to-basics planning and strategy implementation, and the employees *know* that he or she believes in it, then *they* will believe in it. Furthermore, a chief executive who is committed will see to it that all the training necessary to *make* a strategy work will find its way into the company budget. The following techniques should be utilized to make planning a part of the firm's everyday operation.

Practice management by objectives (more on this later).
Conduct formal reviews (not hit-or-miss).
Budget reviews (how're we doing?).
Be result-oriented (reward for achievement).
Establish ongoing training programs (learn while you earn).
Integrate long- and short-range plans.

Figure 3.1
Strategic Planning

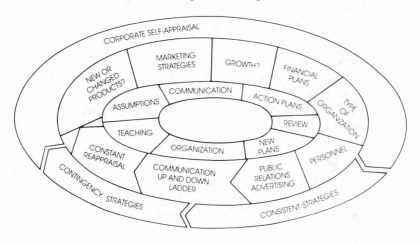

Strategic planning can be made to have bottom-line impact. Effective top managers can guarantee its success if they carefully develop strategies and take the proper steps to ensure their implementation. In fact, if your organization is to be successful over a period of time, it really has *no other alternative*. Remember, the future is always now.

CHECKLIST FOR STRATEGIC PLANNING
"Where do we go from here?"

There was a film some years ago called *If It's Tuesday, This Must Be Belgium*. It was a funny movie about the inevitability of absolute planning in a world that was (sort of) totally predictable.

We should all live so long. Nothing is that predictable.

Basic strategic planning in an exciting but unpredictable world means we should be questioning ourselves constantly. *Strategy* (that military word involved with winning) is important, is at the heart of *any* plan you will ever write and is the key to answering the question of where your venture goes from here. The following are some of the questions you will want to ask yourself as you make strategic planning an integral part of your managerial style:

- Do we need new or changed products to meet our competition?
- Do our marketing strategies get our products/services to the customer efficiently?
- Have we analyzed our growth in light of our future needs?
- Do we have a clear strategy for financing the present and future?
- Does "form follow function" in our organization planning?
- Does our personnel plan meet the needs of our company's objectives and strategies?
- Do our public relations and advertising plans support all our major strategies?
- Do we know our corporate destiny? What is our real business?
- Are we consistent in all our strategies? Have we removed all the conflicts?
- Do we have contingency strategies in place, through

reappraisal, monitoring and reviewing?
- Are our strategies communicated to all our key decision-making managers?
- Are our assumptions (premises) communicated to all our managers?
- Have we all agreed on action plans, and are they in place?
- Do we teach the planning principles on a regular basis to all our supervisory and managerial staff?
- Are we result-oriented? Do we reward achievement?

4 THE MARKETING PLAN

"Hear ye, hear ye, here comes the peddler!"

For the back-to-basics planner, marketing is not some strange, mysterious art. It's been done from the beginning of time. One can just picture an aggressive Cro-Magnon fellow painting appetizing cuts of antelope and succulent roots on the rocks outside his cave if he wanted to trade them with passing travelers for warm winter furs or a new set of bone needles.

Broadsides and banners were used to proclaim performances of entertainers or hawk wares back before the average person could read. And we all delight in the mortar and pestle of the pharmacist, the boot outside the cobbler's shop and the red and white barber pole (lest we forget that the barber once doubled as the local surgeon).

That's marketing.

Selling a product or service is what marketing is all about.

THE PRODUCT

If a product or service isn't fundamentally good or needed, the world's greatest marketing effort is doomed to fail. While the case can be made that hula hoops and pet rocks were not "needed" products, they still made their creators quite rich. That brings up the point that marketing can create a need for something when such a need did not previously exist. But be reminded, those fads were not long-lived. The need was not real.

As a back-to-basics planner, your ultimate goal in planning is to build for long-term growth. The first priority is therefore a *good product or service.*

THE CONSUMER

What do you know about the consumer—current or intended—for your product? In the marketing plan, everything you know about the consumer determines where you should plan to position your product.

Remember, *every* business has competition. In this era of shrinking personal budgets and tightening disposable incomes, consumers are getting smarter, more selective and harder to persuade (or change from current buying habits). Moreover, consumers are being bombarded by too many impressions (Advertising Council estimates are about 1,500 per day) of goods and services to make a judgment on instinct and impulse alone. You, the back-to-basics planner, must use your tools to devise a plan that will help consumers make those decisions.

Therefore (aside from the value of the product itself), marketing becomes the single *most important* thing you will do to guarantee long life to your venture.

THE MARKETING PLAN

There are some who will say that the marketing plan *is* your business plan. If you fail in planning, developing and producing your goods or services, or in attracting customers for them, there is no business. To the extent that your operation's sales/revenue projections are derived from the success or failure of your marketing plans, that is correct. And to the extent that your volume and productivity of that product are the driving engine of your "variable costs," your expenses and, ultimately, the bottom line of profits or losses are mightily influenced by your marketing plan.

But we must make the distinction. Marketing is the basic element of a business plan. It is *not* of itself a business plan. Marketing is a way to move your products and services from your warehouse, your office, or your shop into the lives of the consumer. The back-to-basics marketing plan is a *way* to get there—spelled out in detail, with specifics of *what* you will move, *how* you will move it and the target *consumer* to whom it will be sold.

A number of methods are available to the back-to-basics marketing planner to make the intended consumer aware of a product or service. The following are but a few:

- The "tune-in" ad. Radio and television networks use them all the time to remind listeners and viewers of upcoming programming. Why? To capture consumer interest, to make consumers tune in, to increase the audience share, to sell commercial time on those programs for more money than the competition is getting.

- Print media advertising. Newspapers and magazines present the product or service to get the consumer to *try* something new or to continue *buying* a familiar product or service.

- The commercial. We are now an electronic generation. We know more about commercials than any society in history. (When a slogan from a hamburger commercial pops up in a presidential campaign, we have reached the apogee of commercial saturation.) But with all the criticism, commercials *work*.

- Direct mail. The U.S. Postal Service has become a partner in marketing services in this country. It brings to our doors every day marketing inducements to try a new product, retry an old product, stock up on an old friend, take advantage of a discount. (Discount couponing, albeit venerable, is the fastest-growing marketing tool in America today.)

- Publicity events. "Live at Kennedy Center," sponsored sports awards competitions, as well as competitions and awards in other fields are all marketing events.

They bring together people who have a particular interest, and while those people are there, they become *aware* of a company, a product, a service. In order to choose the best method to create appropriate consumer awareness, the back-to-basics planner knows not only the product but also its intended market. Before an effective back-to-basics marketing plan is written, these two key variables must be examined.

THE BACK-TO-BASICS PLANNER'S MARKETING TACTICS

The back-to-basics planner uses the resources available to learn every feature of the product or service to be marketed. Once the "goods" are defined, the "consumers" must be defined. To accomplish this task, let's take a look at the various marketing tactics the back-to-basics planner can employ:

Market and Marketing Research. Market research is research conducted to establish the extent and location of a market for a product or service. It determines whether or not your concept is viable and whether or not the dollars you plan to put into it will have a suitable return. It is the gathering of *factual* information regarding consumer or user preferences.

To establish an important distinction in terminology: market research is the *action*; marketing research is the result of the action.

Advertising. Advertising is simply the publishing or announcing of *news* via paid messages.

Don't let your friends look down their noses at you when you call advertising news. The fact is, when a consumer hears about a product or service, particularly for the first time, it *is* news—albeit paid for. It is the opportunity, however, for you to present your message the way you want it to be said rather than have someone else say it for you. That's a very important "plus" for anybody involved in selling.

Sales approach. The sales approach varies depending on the services being sold. It can be as simple as the newspaper stand at the subway or bus stop or as complex as the movement of 20 consumer home products from a major manufacturer. It can involve one person, teams or battalions of sales representatives.

Sales approaches include personal sales, mail order, point-of-sale and many variations. While the techniques vary, the result is basic: movement of products or services to the consumer.

Merchandising. Merchandising is a sales-promotion activity, usually oriented more toward advertising than toward sales. Merchandising relates to couponing, the two-fer discounting in the theater, and other discounting activities, often in conjunction with some other business. (A fast-food chain might offer a discount on an entertainment complex, for instance.) The purpose of merchandising is to induce the consumer to make multiple purchases, usually in different products or services.

Public relations. Public relations is the business of inducing the public to have an understanding of and goodwill toward a person, service, institution or product. Said another way, public relations involves those activities designed to develop images for products or services.

It is the ability to have a medium or the media report on your activities in a positive way—unpaid. It is important to realize, however, that there is a *quid pro quo:* The medium involved must be convinced that your story is of concern to its audience—that is, the public interest must be satisfied. The event must be worth reporting from the medium's point of view, not just yours. The persuasive (and creative) ability required for that is worth a lot in your PR budget.

Publicity. Publicity is an act designed to attract public interest. Free advertising, if you will. "Hype." It's a good flak beating a drum. It should be noted that good, imaginative writing is crucial for effective publicists. More often than not, when their material is used, it is because it has been presented in a press release in an interesting and well-written way, and a beleaguered editor will use it for "filler" or "lead" because his or her audience will find it interesting.

MARKETING PHILOSOPHY

Marketing is a continuum. It is not something that you do at a particular point and then discontinue. That does not mean that a back-to-basics plan is cast in stone. But it does mean that a marketing plan, like all plans, is an organic instrument dedicated to the long-term life of the venture.

Product Life Cycle

We've all heard the phrase *product life cycle*. A product starts, rises to a level, holds at a certain share and then, perhaps, starts a decline.

There are (usually) many years of life in a product, albeit at varying stages of health. Part of your job in marketing planning is to tailor programs for the different stages of that product's life. You will refine how you sell. Part of that depends on the *budget* that is available. Generally, you have more money at the start of the product's life and have to rely more on imagination and other types of marketing tools as the life cycle proceeds.

We must state our belief again that, in this day and age, research is the indispensable ingredient. Given the education and fragmentation of interests of the American buying public, launching a marketing campaign without research is simply like a blind person struggling through a swamp.

So we get to *budgets*. Be sure you budget enough for research—as well as for sufficient *advertising* and aggressive *publicity*. The truth of the matter is that there is a lot of competition out there, and you've got to have enough drums to beat.

Without belaboring the issue, we would recommend that merchandising be used sparingly or *not at all*, when launching a new product. That is, we don't believe in discounting or couponing at the beginning of a product's life. We know that flies in the face of a lot of current marketing practices, but in our view, the "I can get it for you wholesale" approach, as it were, diminishes the image of the product—cheapens it, perhaps—at the very beginning of its life. Later in its life, when the product needs a boost, couponing or other merchandising techniques could be helpful, but not when you're first building its image.

This does not refer, of course, to sampling (you know, those little tubes of toothpaste or hand cream that arrive in your mailbox unexpectedly). Sampling has always been a great way to launch a new product. (The method has drawbacks, of course, with services.)

Coupons Versus Samples

What is the track record of coupons versus samples? Is there a difference in cost between these two approaches? Is one more effective than the other? The answer is yes.

Larger product companies—the Colgate-Palmolives, the Procter & Gambles—obviously use every available kind of marketing technique to move their products. But when it comes to the question of coupons versus sampling, sampling is more cost-effective.

It's obviously cheaper to give away pieces of paper than it is to give away samples of the product. However, when you weigh the cost of coupons or the cost of sample product against the number of times the person uses the product during its life cycle, it becomes apparent that sampling is far and away the most effective approach to marketing a new product.

Not true, however, in marketing a mature product! Couponing and many other means are more effective in that case.

ELEMENTS OF THE BACK-TO-BASICS MARKETING PLAN

Concept

Marketing all starts with a concept. How does a concept start? It starts with experience, with vision, with imagination, with a knowledge of trends; it all starts with an *idea*.

But maybe the idea stinks. You *could* be wrong. Perhaps no one needs a new flavor of toothpaste this year or a new production of *King Lear* or a pet rock that crawls. What's your next step?

You need a start-up budget.

But you're saying, "Hey, wait a minute. I thought a budget was the *last* thing you do in a plan!"

That's right. The budget *is* the last thing you do in developing the total strategic and operational plan for your venture. But then what do you need a start-up budget for?

Market Research

Just a few thousand dollars, a simple market research program—focus groups, interviews led by moderators, mail-in questionnaires, telephone surveys—is money well-spent at the beginning of your venture. Remember, *you* don't do it; you let someone else do it. You lay out a concept, write up a simple statement about the public you think is your target and hire a professional to do the work. It will be the best money you ever spent.

What does market research do? It lets you know whether or not you're a genius.

- It may confirm your *concept*. Or it may say you're a genius if you modify the concept in certain ways. Or it may tell you to abandon the idea altogether.
- It can help define the *areas of interest* in the product or service. Who? Where? In what form? With what modifications?
- It can even help establish *pricing parameters*. How much will people pay for what you're offering? Is it too low or too high? Can you make money within those parameters?
- It can help *locate the market*. This can make your particular demographics more specific. And those specific demographics can be related to the wealth of demographic information now available. This not only has impact on the targets of your advertising and promotional campaigns but is a great aid to the copywriters and advertising people who have to communicate the message.
- It can help *identify your competition*. (What else are people buying that will compete with your product?)

Product Development

If the marketing research tells you it's a "go," now the development people join the team. (Notice that we did not say, "the development people take over." You're building a team for the long life of the venture; no one goes off and works alone; right? Right.)

Successful product planning follows a basic outline, which we addressed as early as the Introduction to this book and which has been used by all the great companies.

- *Logic*. There is consensus among all concerned that the new product or service is logical; marketing agrees that there is a need, development says that it can be created, finance says that the funds are available, and marketing and finance have agreed on pricing and have arrived at a suitable ROI.

- *Design.* This is where those creative talents come into play. However, be sure they design what the market said was needed!
- *Prototypes.* Build as many as necessary. Remember the space program and all those rockets that fizzled on the launch pad? Oh, my, it was depressing. But remember the day John Glenn orbited the earth? The prototypes were important to everyone—not the least of whom was John Glenn.
- *Manufacturing sample.* This is where your production and operations people really shine. If they can't make the sample cost-effective and guarantee it during the life of the product, then you've reached another plateau until they can (your product is on "hold").
- *Quality control.* In the whole marketing and development process, you are concerned with establishing procedures that will give you quality control throughout the life of the product. The consumer expects to get the same product time after time after time.

Financial Plan Budgeting

These financial plans and budgets are not to be confused with those that you will submit for the operational plan (see Chapter 6) relating to your entire venture.

These financial plans and budgets are primarily in the purview of the marketing director. Depending on the venture (that is, whether you are manufacturing personal computers, managing a theater, providing counseling services), the types of expenses and what you call them will vary; but they generally fall into the categories discussed in the following paragraphs.

- *Cost of goods/services.* Your real concern in this area is *pricing.* It's probable that when Bill Blass creates a one-of-a kind dress for a valued client, he doesn't concern himself too much with the cost of production in setting the price, but a dress house on Fashion Avenue is very concerned about the total cost of each piece before the price is set. We go into more detail on this in the chapter on quantifying, but this is where development, production, finance and marketing must be in total agreement and have no secrets. The price placed on the goods or services must provide a healthy gross profit so that there will be a net profit when other expenses are deducted. Marketing departments (meaning advertising, promotion, public relations, merchandising) must know the leeway (and ground rules) under which they operate: Do they discount? Can they offer group reductions? Do they sample? Is there a suggested price or a firm price? Does the offering go to the top-of-the-line demographic, or is the outreach more general? Well, you see the importance for the back-to-basics marketing plan of firming up pricing.

- *Departmental budgets.* Departmental budgets become a part of the overall consolidated plan. Each department in the marketing area must have a budget for the year.

- *Media costs.* There will be figures later in the chapter illustrating the media schedule. But the media costs can be as much as 15 percent of the total costs of your operation. How much do you plan to spend on television, radio, newspapers, magazines, merchandising, promotional events, giveaways, etc.?

   It should be obvious that the financial plan for marketing should not be done "by guess and by God." It is basic to the success of the venture.

- *Sales.* In many companies sales and marketing are a part of the same department, but in many others, they are separate operations. There is a marketing department at Macy's (and other large department store chains) that handles the elements we have discussed, but there is also a huge sales staff of people who deal face-to-face with the public daily. Ford Motor Company has a large marketing department, but you buy your cars from a salesperson on the floor of a showroom, generally owned by a private dealer/entrepreneur, not Ford Motor Company. IBM has always marketed and sold its own products directly to the customer, but even IBM is now distributing those products through non-IBM dealers.

   How to plan a sales campaign, motivate and reward salespeople and utilize buyer input for further development of product and sales are the topics for a whole series of other books. For the purposes of developing a back-to-basics marketing plan, it is important to remember that the planning of those sales and the accounting of them on a regular and orderly basis is the basic monitoring of your marketing plan.

The advent of the computer has made it possible to track every conceivable kind of sales today. Ticket sales can be tracked by zip code and therefore by demographics. Product sales can be tracked by price, color, size, model, volume, etc., making it possible to set up reasonable manufacturing and distribution schedules. Services can be tracked by location, price, number, volume and type, allowing the company to anticipate staffing needs and service problems.

The data are available to enable you to *satisfy the customer*. It's a marketer's dream.

Advertising

In the nineteenth century, advertising appeared mostly in newspapers, catalogs and broadsides. Those were also the days when signs on hotels read, "Dogs, actors and drummers not welcome."

Well, we've come a long way. Dogs are welcome in a lot of places, and actors and sales/advertising people are acceptable in polite society.

Frankly, our society has now reached the point where the train of commerce is pulled by the engine of advertising. Although you may discount or pooh-pooh it, you as a consumer still use advertising to help you make many of your selections. Admit it! Why this dependence on advertising? Because advertising is *news* (albeit slanted) that you need to know.

There's no secret to the advertising section of your back-to-basics marketing plan; it just involves hard work. And it's basic. The following paragraphs outline some of the key decisions you will have to make regarding your advertising campaign.

- *Positioning, strategy, copy.* One of the most interesting books in recent years, by Al Ries and Jack Trout, is called *Positioning: The Battle for Your Mind*. The authors contend that positioning is what you do to the mind of the prospect. They use as examples, "Avis is only No. 2 in rent-a-cars, so why go with us? *We try harder.*" "Honeywell, the other computer company." "Seven-Up: The *uncola.*"

Positioning is spending the time and research money necessary to find the positions (the *holes*) in the marketplace. Once you've found the niche where your product or service can fit, fill a need and make a profit, you develop the *strategy* to teach the public, to reach the minds of viewers, listeners, readers, convincing them (1) that the hole *exists* and (2) that *you* can fill it.

The *copy* you write, the images you create, the slogan you promote pound at that *idea* day after day after day.

- *Choice of media.* Your research has given you information regarding who and where your customers are. The selection of media relates directly to that information. Someone once asked a famous bank robber (following his capture, prosecution and conviction) why he had robbed banks. His answer: "Because that's where the money is."

Obviously, you advertise *where the people are*—making sure that the people you are going after are the people you *want.*

Later, we will present some forms that will help you create your media plan. For now, remember that your options are:

Print, broadcast, cable
Direct mail, mail order
Freestanding inserts, flyers
Couponing, samples

- *Length of campaign.* Allocating resources on a calendar basis is fundamental to the effectiveness of your advertising. You will do a lot of strategic analysis and "skull" sessions with the advertising agency, R&D and production in order to get the "most bang for the buck," by building awareness, creating need, sampling, and attempting to create ingrained buying habits.

- *Budgeting.* Cost per thousand will undoubtedly be the criterion for your allocation of resources by medium. But rely heavily on the demographic information available from each medium so that you can be very selective about your audience and your expenditures. You may want to focus your efforts like a rifle shot rather than scatter them like a shotgun blast.

- *Staffing.* Most companies hire agencies to handle their advertising needs. A few have their own in-house staffs. Some go to full-service agencies; others buy from "boutiques." Your decision of whether to do it all, do none or do some will be based on dollars (the agency gets 15 percent of billing plus expenses and production costs), on the character of your company (do you need ads in a real hurry, like Macy's?), on the scope of your campaigns, on the talents you can attract and on the buying power you as a company may have compared to the buying/bargaining power of the agency. Whatever you decide, staffing considerations are a part of your job when creating the advertising part of the plan.

ISSUES TO STUDY IN DEVELOPING A MARKETING PLAN

In 1981 David S. Hopkins did a survey of 267 major American firms regarding the elements they consider in developing a marketing plan. It was published by the Conference Board, and the elements are listed below in order of priority.

1. Forecast of market demand
2. Market share of business
3. Competitive strengths/weaknesses
4. Competitors' market share
5. Market segmentation
6. Customers' changing needs
7. Technological trends
8. Risk factors
9. Environmental issues
10. Government regulations
11. Alternative strategies
12. Assign product to a matrix position

13.   Contingency plans
14.   Product life-cycle analysis
15.   Postmortem on previous plan

Whether or not you analyze the above elements in the order listed, it seems obvious that you should consider *all* of them, to avoid surprises.

FORMS FOR DEVELOPING THE MARKETING PLAN

This section presents some sample forms that will get you started on the road to a good back-to-basics marketing plan. Other aids are available, and you will design many of your own. However, the use of these fundamental forms will help you incorporate your marketing plan into the overall business plan.

Analysis Matrix

The simple matrix shown in Figure 4.1 is a quick method of analyzing various aspects of your current and future market(s) and aiding you in developing *facts* for your marketing objectives. The matrix can be larger or smaller, as required, and it can be used to analyze many different types of data.

The "Product" column should be used to define the variety of items you offer for sale: the list of brands you produce, the array of services you perform, the number of productions you plan to offer, etc. "Market" can be defined by region, by demographic, by type (consumer, industrial, etc.).

For example, the chart can be used to analyze *Total Sales* (see Figure 4.1) by number of units or in dollars. The products or services would be identified in the left column ("M"). Then a calculation is possible in each of the squares to lay out the sales projections for easy, visual understanding.

The same exercise could be developed for the *Cost of Goods* or *Cost of Sales* for each product/service and market segment.

The chart can also be used to calculate *Gross Profits* on each product/service by market segment, as well as *Marketing Costs*, etc.

There is no magic to this simple chart. It is primarily a visual tool for segmenting elements in order to identify problems and opportunities in your marketing plan.

Figure 4.1
Analysis Matrix:
Total Annual Sales by Market and by Product

Product / Market	P	P	P	P	Annual Total by Market
M					
M					
M					
M					
Annual total by product					

Figure 4.2
Analysis Matrix:
Problems and Opportunities (Defining Responsibility)

Departments / Factors	Marketing	Research and Development	Production	Other Departments
Sociological				
Technological				
Economic				
Environmental				
Political				

Figure 4.2 illustrates the use of an analysis matrix to assess the problems and opportunities facing a venture's marketing effort.

Figure 4.3
Rate of Return Worksheet

Year	Cash Flow (× $1,000)	Market Segmentation	Market Expansion	Discount Rate (%)	Present Value
0					
1					
2					
3					
4					
5					
6					
7					
8					
9					
10					
11					
12					
13					
14					
15					

NOTE: This worksheet is valuable for each product and service you are developing, allowing you to ask the "what if" questions necessary to an effective marketing plan. Should we expand? Should we segment (break out other products or spin-offs)? How will our discounts affect us? And so on.

Figure 4.4
Risk Analysis

Element	Low (0-17%)	Medium (18-49%)	High (50-100%)
Industry			
Maturity			
Competitive position			
Strategy			
Assumptions			
Past performance of unit			
Past performance of management			
Expected level of future performance			
Overall risk			

NOTE: Each "risk" should be listed in percentages as well as identified by name.

Figure 4.5
Marketing Budget Compared to Sales

	1st Quarter	2d Quarter	3d Quarter	4th Quarter	Total
(#) Projected sales ($)	$___ %___	$___ %___	$___ %___	$___ %___	$___ %___
Marketing budget ($)					
Marketing cost/sales	$				

NOTE: The **full** marketing budget (media costs, promotions, staff, production) should be used, and the quarterly percent of total put in each quarterly square. This will give you the true picture of your marketing costs-to-sales in the last line.

Figure 4.6
Media Flowchart by Month

Medium	Jan.	Feb.	March	April	May	June	July	Aug.	Sept.	Oct.	Nov.	Dec.	$	%
Newspapers														
Magazines														
Television														
Radio														
Cable														
Brochures														
Outdoor														
Promotions														
Production														
Advertising spending ($)														
Advertising spending (%)														100.0

NOTE: In practice, you would break this chart down into much finer detail. That is, the chart should be divided by weeks; each week should be dated; television should be divided by network, spot and local, as should radio; magazines should be grouped into national and regional categories; newspapers should be grouped into national or local categories; promotions should be identified. Also, this chart should be done *twice*—once with arrows that readily indicate the mass of coverage at a given time and again with figures indicating the dollar cost of coverage at a given time.

Figure 4.7
Media/Promotional Expenditures by Quarter

Medium	1st Quarter ($)	2d Quarter ($)	3d Quarter ($)	4th Quarter ($)	Total ($)	Percentage of Total
Newspapers						
Magazines						
Television						
Radio						
Cable						
Brochures						
Outdoor						
Promotions						
Production						
TOTAL						
Percentage by quarter						

NOTE: This chart is a Management Summary of the finite detail on Figure 5.6, to be used for analysis and reporting.

Figure 4.8
Promotional Calendar 19___

Month	Project	Start Time	End Time	Type	In Coopera- tion with	Responsibility	Budget

NOTE: This chart helps you set the flow of your promotions and monitor their scope and timeliness.

CHECKLIST FOR THE MARKETING PLAN

"I ain't lost."

There is a story about a man who was traveling in a rural area and needed directions. He found a young boy seated on a log and asked him the road to the nearest telephone. The boy said, "I don't know." "Well, does this road lead to a town?" "I don't know," the boy again replied. The traveler, impatiently: "Does this road lead to a bigger road?" The response: "I don't know." Finally, the man snorted, "You're not very smart, are you?" "Well," replied the boy amiably, "I ain't lost."

Perhaps everyone preparing a back-to-basics marketing plan should have "I ain't lost" tattooed on their eyelids. That's what a marketing plan avoids—getting lost on the way to market.

The preceding tips have been summaries, at best, of the process involved and the tools required to stay on the road and make the sale. It is a complex process, but not mysterious. You will use many more tools than we have provided to achieve a working marketing plan. But these are the fundamental tools to help you form the outline of what you intend to do.

In summary, we'd like to remind you of some of the things we've touched on:

- Selling a product or service is what marketing is all about.
- The first priority is a *good* product or service—value received for value given.
- What you know about your consumer is the most important piece of information in a good marketing plan.
- Marketing is the way you move your products and services to your consumers. It involves *what* you will move, *how* you will move it and *whom* you will target.
- Marketing defines your message.
- Building *awareness* is your first step. Perception is reality.
- In building that awareness, *control* of the message is why you employ advertising, publicity, public relations. Don't depend on anyone else.
- Marketing researchers are the "first among equals." They give you the *facts* from which you work.
- Market research is the action; marketing research is the

result of the action.
- Advertising is paid news. Believe it or not, consumers want to know what's out there on the market.
- Merchandising is usually designed to induce the consumer to make multiple purchases.
- Public relations is the controlled way to develop images for products, services or institutions.
- Publicity is activity designed to attract public interest.
- Marketing is a continuum. Like all plans, the back-to-basics marketing plan is an organic instrument concerned with the long-term life of the venture.
- Remember the acronym *BAP*. To launch a marketing plan and keep up with the product's life cycle, you must combine budgets, advertising, and publicity in an orderly way.
- Sampling is very cost-effective in launching a new product.
- The first step is a start-up budget to do initial market research (remember, the indispensable ingredient).
- Research helps you clarify your concept, define the areas of interest, establish pricing parameters, locate the market and identify your competition.
- Product planning follows the process of logic, design, prototypes, manufacturing sample, quality control.
- The marketing budget must take into account cost of goods/ services, pricing, departmental budgets, media costs.
- In planning advertising you are concerned with positioning, strategy, copy, choice of media, length of campaign, budgeting, cost per thousand and staffing.

5 THE ORGANIZATION PLAN

"Unity is plural and at minimum is two."
—Richard Buckminister Fuller

How many times have you heard someone in your organization refer to it as a "team"? While it must be confessed that modern managements are very concerned with "team spirit"—that is, building a staff that is enthusiastic about working together for a common goal—the use of sports analogies is a misnomer when it comes to the structure of American business.

American business is typically organized just like the American military. Think about it for a minute. Pull out your company's organization chart. There are a lot of little squares on the bottom, which report to still fewer little squares above them, which report to one big square at the top. (See Figure 5.1.) Whether you call them presidents, vice-presidents, directors, managers and supervisors or whether you call them generals, colonels, majors, captains, lieutenants and sergeants, everybody has a boss, everybody is in a square, and everybody reports to somebody.

The "typical" American business organization chart is a holdover from the "good old days" when owner/entrepreneurs ran the place to suit themselves and created a structure based on what they were most familiar with—the military.

Figure 5.1
Military/Corporate
Organizational Structure

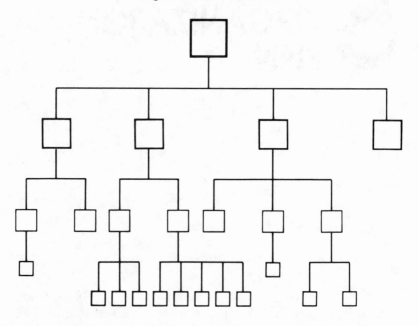

In the past 50 years there has been enormous change in the way those organizations are run, with the people in the little boxes being allowed much more flexibility and greater participation. For instance, the change of "personnel departments" to "human resources departments" involves more than semantics. It is a recognition of human needs and a sign of flexibility in business in the twentieth century. But despite the change in the *manner* in which organizations are run, the *structure* of those organizations (as reflected by the organization charts) remains fixed in a form that West Point would admire.

We have heard a lot about "quality circles" lately, first as they are practiced in Japan and now as they are tentatively being explored by a growing number of enlightened American businesses. There is no secret to their success. In the quality-circles approach, a problem (whatever it is) is tackled with an allocation of resources, particularly people, from as many departments as are interested and/ or involved. Quality circles represent the allocation of human resources according to *task*, not according to department or direct reporting relationship on the organization chart. (See Figure 5.2.)

There is an irony to all the hoopla about Japanese quality circles. When, seemingly overnight, the Japanese came to dominate us with their automobile and electronics sales, some frantic U.S. managers started looking for the secret to their success. Problem solving, employee input, employee loyalty and dedication as exemplified by the quality-circles approach became the rallying cry of self-defense and change.

The irony is that America had a crack at it first. In 1966 Warren G. Bennis, in *Changing Organization*, wrote a landmark work on the changes necessary in organization and personnel management in the last half of the twentieth century. One paragraph is particularly prescient:

> Allow me to leapfrog to the conclusions of my paper now. It is my premise that the bureaucratic form of organization is out of joint with contemporary realities, that new shapes, patterns, and models are emerging which promise drastic changes in the conduct of the corporation and the managerial practices in general. In the next 25 to 50 years we should witness and participate in the end of bureaucracy as we know it and the rise of new social systems better suited to twentieth century demands of industrialization.

The changes from industrialization to technology and to the communications world in which we currently live can also be inferred in Bennis's conclusion. He *did* see change, and the so-called quality circles are only a small part of that change. What we are really hearing in his prediction is a need for *flexibility* in organizations that allows their form to change as the task evolves—always utilizing, preserving, developing and expanding the greatest of all natural resources, the human being.

In America we call it management by objectives (MBO). Coined from a phrase used by Dr. Kurt Lewin in World War II in his

Figure 5.2
The Quality Circles Structure

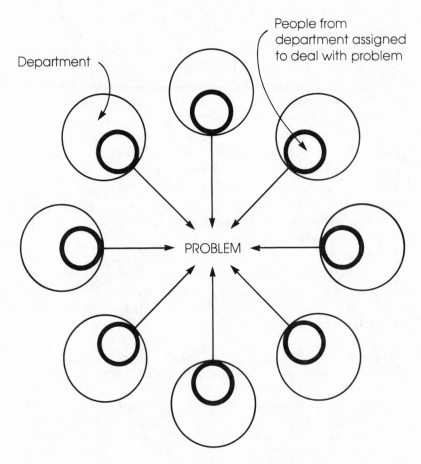

study of housewives' buying habits and then codified by Peter Drucker, MBO has become the subject of many books and the touchstone of many successful businesses in this country.

MANAGEMENT BY OBJECTIVES

While there is no such thing as a *perfect* or *absolute* organization tool, management by objectives is the most logical choice for a company or enterprise that wishes to run its operation based on sound business practices and good business planning.

The architects of the 1920s taught us, by theory and through the example of some of the most extraordinary buildings ever built, that "form follows function." While fads in architecture ebb and flow, giving us everything from upended ice trays to Sheraton breakfront crowns, the best, the most satisfying, the most functional and the most enduring structures never depart from the formula—form follows function. You build a building based on how it is to be *used*. Grace, beauty, imagination, utility, endurance are not excluded from the formula, nor are they grafted on. Rather, the basic purpose forces the creation of a unified whole.

Such should be the case in organization planning—form should follow function. People and tasks should not be made to fit into predetermined squares; tasks should dictate the people, their place on the chart and their function as well as their relationships to other people on the chart. While it would be unwise to describe such a chart as a bowl of moving goldfish, with its members acting at will upon each other, it does not seem farfetched to describe it as an anthill, seemingly running amok before our eyes but actually one of the most highly organized societies in nature, with its members functioning both together and separately toward common and necessary goals in a constant ebb and flow of effort. Flexibility, then, has become crucial in planning during these last years of the twentieth century and is a fundamental element in management and management by objectives.

Management by objectives is the management of people. MBO helps define where all of you want to go (the goal) and how you can get there (the strategies), and it provides a quantitative measurement of the target and your progress in reaching it.

That paragraph is so similar to the description of how you write your business plan that you must be scratching your head and wondering if we accidentally reprinted a passage from an earlier chapter. No. You can't plan a company's goals without people, and you can't manage and inspire people without involving them in the company's goals.) MBO is a circle (albeit perhaps not a quality circle): Form follows function, people make a company, companies give people purpose.

If you plan to institute management by objectives as your company's method of organization and personnel planning, there are three ways you can go about it:

- *Objectives.* In this approach you work with your managers to set objectives over and above what they currently do. You use this approach to stretch the managers (and their departments' contribution) in an orderly and targeted way.
- *Total planning process.* Here you incorporate personnel goals with corporate goals; the organizational structure becomes part of the business-planning process of the organization on a year-to-year basis.
- *Completely new way of looking at your organization.* In this approach MBO goes beyond the annual business-planning process and addresses the future of the organization, its purpose, its people, its training; MBO becomes an integral part of the strategic planning of an operation and truly takes the ebb and flow of that anthill and turns it into the ebb and flow of the tides themselves. It assumes a complete reorientation of company procedures; it makes a different set of assumptions about the nature of people in an organization and how they are to be utilized; and it assures a change in the delegation of responsibility.

Let us say right now that there is no "correct" choice among the foregoing three options. (The fact that we think you should choose at least one of the options should be self-evident.) The nature of your venture, its position in the competitive world today, the composition of your work force and your commitment to business planning as an orderly process will all dictate the choice you make as to which of the three ways you will go. You know best whether your company is ready for the third option. You may want to begin with the first approach, to stretch your people and prepare them for the future. You may be far enough along in orderly business planning to go with the second approach and incorporate your human resources goals into your business-planning goals on an annual basis. This chapter makes no assumptions about which way you will choose to go. But we would like to share with you some of the procedures and processes that will help you make the choices.

ALLOCATION OF MANAGEMENT TIME

Everyone is involved in management—of people, of money, of resources, of departments. We have great respect for both presidents and telephone operators, sales managers and typists. They *all* manage something. As the first exercise in MBO, it is necessary to analyze (together!) how much time is spent managing and how much time is spent doing.

We are always fearful of generic charts; they tend to simplify complicated functions and minimize human potential. But they can help us organize our thoughts about what we're *supposed* to be doing (as opposed to what we are *probably* doing). The only thing that everyone in the world shares is *time*. The rational and effective allocation of our time for business, for family, for society and for ourselves is our major goal in life. By looking at Figure 5.3, you can tell (in general terms) whether or not you are channeling your business time in a meaningful and effective way, both for yourself and for your company. It is the first step in the long process of defining the objectives of management and of each employee in an MBO program.

Figure 5.3
The Allocation of Time at
Various Organizational Levels

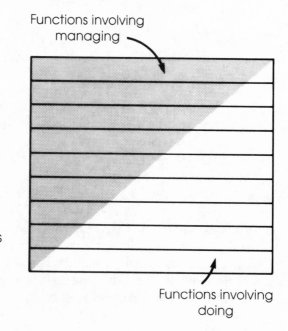

Functions involving
managing

President

Vice-President

Director

Manager

Supervisor

Group Leaders

Staff/Team

Skilled Professionals

Workers

Functions involving
doing

MANAGEMENT PHILOSOPHY

This next exercise should probably be done in private. If, as we contend, everyone manages *something*, how we manage *people* becomes our most important function. We credit Douglas McGregor in *The Human Side of Enterprise* for the chart shown in Figure 5.4.

Figure 5.4
Management Style

Style	X	Y
Assumptions	People are lazy and need to be prodded to get them to work	People are creators of work and become highly committed and self-directed
Actions	Control, direct	Delegate, advise, provide resources
Appraisal of performance	Tell and sell	Listen and help

Before we go further, let us refer back to our list of options for implementing MBO. The state of your company *now* will help determine your choice. The people *currently* on your payroll will influence that choice. We have seen tests done on management style that were enough to make you weep. Managers have given examples in which the "Y" management style was easy—and indeed, was the desired method—even without the institution of formal MBO. However, they were also managing people (many of whom they had not hired) for whom the "Y" management style came across as a sign of weakness. These employees had tenure, they seemed set in their ways, and they had long-standing connections with a management that was reluctant to change either their status or their authority. In short, many factors were at work in these cases to make a manager both an "X" and a "Y." Such situations aren't hopeless, but they can sure look that way to an enthusiastic and enlightened manager.

What is the solution? Define the problem. We refer back to Chapter 1: if management has a fundamental commitment to good back-to-basics business planning and organization based on MBO, the atmosphere will be one of enthusiasm and invention; if there is reluctance, even of a subtle nature, the process is doomed as a companywide endeavor. This latter situation presents an opportunity for the enlightened manager to use MBO where it will work and wait for its success to convince management to use it elsewhere. MBO can be threatening to many people who like the "old ways." Without universal agreement (particularly at the top), MBO will not work throughout an enterprise. But it can still work in limited areas. Try it. Its success *can* win friends and influence people. (Said another way, MBO can be successful in an open and enlightened environment, but unfortunately, sometimes a manager has no choice but to "control and direct" because participation and support are limited or nonexistent. Don't be discouraged. Make MBO work where possible. The ripples can spread.)

WHAT IS MBO WORTH?

Why should you even bother with all this? MBO sounds like a lot of work; what's the payoff? Thousands of companies have instituted MBO since the 1950s. They continue to use it. The reasons why can be summed up as follows:

- MBO provides the greatest flexibility in managing and directing people in an enterprise, allowing a venture to remain highly competitive in a constantly changing world.
- It is a system that permits a manager to become more involved and committed to the enterprise; it allows managers to manage and all employees to feel themselves a part of the process.
- Everyone is a part of the organization, its goals, its purposes, under MBO. Their commitment and devotion are based on something besides payday.
- If everyone is an important part of the process of a venture, and they *know* that they are, they have a greater stake in its success and profitability. Books such as *In Search of Excellence* deal with companies that are successful because

they create a certain atmosphere and standard of excellence; those companies have very highly evolved, long-term organization- and personnel-planning processes that have contributed mightily to their success and profitability.

THE FUTURE IS NOW

Are you getting bored with hearing that "The future is now"? Don't be. The acceleration of events, technology and human confusion/frustration dictate that we carry the thought with us always; we forget it at our peril.

In the work of Warren Bennis in 1966, from which we quoted earlier, he identified some of the events "down the road" that were expected to influence our interpersonal relationships in business in the future:

- We'll be working in teams—more in interdependent relationships than in direct-report/carry-out-the-duty relationships.
- Our life-styles will change—and we must learn to manage that change, accept it and accept people who are new and different (in terms of race, sex, age or handicap) into the marketplace as competitive participants.
- We will have more large-scale enterprises, and the growth of the conglomerate necessitates a viable system of delegation. The all-knowing "boss" may go the way of the dinosaurs.
- We are a young working nation—50 percent of the workforce will be under 30, and their needs and acculturization will have an enormous impact on the workplace. (Here Bennis can be forgiven for one error; in 1966 he was unable to predict the lengthening of workers' productive years and the change of the compulsory retirement age to 70; this will have a considerable effect on the workplace and on the institution of changes in systems and procedures in the coming years.)
- We will become a more educated society—which creates a challenging and stimulating environment for managers and employees alike. This is an environment where change and experimentation *should* be possible.

In his discussion of work values, Bennis wrote, "People will be more intellectually committed to their jobs and will probably require more *involvement, participation* and *autonomy* in their work" (emphasis added). Those three principles, which will be discussed at length in the next section, have become the bedrock of the institution of new organization- and personnel-planning systems. The rest of our work in this chapter will be devoted to them.

The world that Bennis described, with a few exceptions, has arrived basically intact. It has created a new kind of environment, where the intellect rather than the muscles are engaged, where complication of tasks necessitates a great deal of delegation and autonomy, and where problem solving will be done by teams or task forces. He called them "temporary organizations," but we recognize such groups in some of our companies today.

An organization with flexibility and the ability to function even under constant change is the goal of the company of the 1980s and 1990s and beyond.

THE THREE PILLARS OF MBO

As stated above, there are three basic premises upon which all useful and productive management by objectives programs are based: involvement, participation and autonomy.

Involvement. From design of the job description to performance review and reward, the employee is completely involved in the job to be done: *what* is to be done, *how* it is to be done, authority for doing it and responsibility (for better or worse) in accounting for its execution. The involvement is complete. That is, the manager does not write the job description and ask the employee to "sign off" on it; the employee writes the job description, using standard guidelines provided by the company, and the manager and the employee rework it until both are satisfied that it is accurate. This same mutuality of effort is apparent in every aspect of the employee's work. Just as the arrows in the pyramid don't go in only one direction (down from on high), so the communication and involvement flow *both* ways, commencing from the bottom.

Participation. Between departments and among people within any given department, there is a need for constant communication to resolve conflicts and elicit mutual consent for all the activities crucial to each person and group. This participation is fundamental to the MBO concept.

Autonomy. Under MBO the employee has both responsibility and authority to succeed or fail. The employee meets with the manager for advice, training and guidance; but they usually communicate only at the end of a performance cycle, when the task(s) are completed. This, logically, gives the manager more time to manage, to think, to plan, rather than hover over employees monitoring their every move.

It is important to remember that you should avoid *superficial* and *nonconnected* programs. Doing something just for show or setting up an isolated project as a kind of prototype in limbo is not a satisfactory way of launching MBO programs. MBO organization planning coupled with a back-to-basics business plan with objectives and strategies is the best way of *guaranteeing a payoff.* And the payoff—rewards, satisfaction, feedback, seeing results—is what the working environment should be all about.

PAYOFF

The payoff occurs when the personnel policies and procedures interconnect directly with our organization planning. There is no organization without people; people function within an organization, either by design or by improvisation; function is the fundamental definition of a business. Ergo, your personnel planning cannot be done withour organization planning, and both organization planning and function rely upon your personnel policies and procedures.

Let's look at another chart, this one on the functions of management (Figure 5.5). Many companies and organizations use the same words and principles: Sometimes they're shown in the form of a ladder (like here); sometimes it's a circle; sometimes it's the four sides of a square, interconnected. Regardless of the format, the underlying concept involves the functions performed by management, based on the principles of MBO.

If you have read the book straight through to this point, you will find the information shown in the Figure very familiar. It is directly related—in fact, it almost exactly corresponds—to the

Figure 5.5
Functions of Management

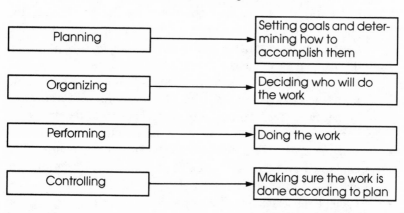

principles of back-to-basics business planning we have discussed before. The interconnection of process and purpose must, by now, be very obvious.

WHAT TYPES OF PEOPLE CAN SLOW YOU DOWN?

What kinds of people can be stumbling blocks to a successful MBO program? We touched on this topic earlier when we talked about instituting a partial MBO program rather than abandoning the idea altogether in firms that aren't yet ready for a companywide program.

- *Too busy.* We all know these people; they're too busy to start anything new. (They are also usually too busy to get their current work done.)
- *Go on without me.* These folks are happy to see us try to make something work, but don't count on their cooperation. Progress is particularly difficult if these people are managers.
- *Perfectionists.* They will rework the nitpicking fine points of the program until it dies of overpolishing, overmodification, excessive detail the first time around.
- *Cast in stone.* Once a plan is written, say these recalcitrants,

never change it, never modify it, never be flexible. Of course, no improvement is possible under such conditions.

- *Copycats.* They copy, right down to the last detail, the plans of some other department or company, so, of course, their plan bears no relation to the needs of this particular department or company.
- *I've always done it that way.* People of this mind-set see no need for change because the old ways are the best ways. Sometimes that's true, but they'll never know for sure, because they never give anything new a chance.
- *Tell me again.* These folks need everything explained and explained and explained. By the time the explanations are exhausted, it's too late to implement the plan.
- *I don't understand.* These people will get hung up on clarifying or tinkering with some particular part of the plan and remain hanging there forever. They'll never see the whole picture.

AVOID THE PITFALLS

Don't let people and problems get in the way of launching the MBO project. Be forewarned and be prepared. Here are some useful strategies:

- Check the progress of your plan on a regular basis, paying particular attention to those people (or types) who can create pitfalls. Be alert for them and look specifically for any signs of problems.
- Define the problem (or person) and analyze the source. Be objective and thorough.
- Look at your options. What are your limitations? What are the opportunities to remove those limitations? Is the problem incurable, or can you devise some training strategies?
- Initiate an alternate plan to bring the recalcitrants aboard or start over with a new tack or a fresh approach.

QUESTIONS FOR MANAGERS

As in the overall company planning process, organization planning works only if everyone is involved, participating and exercising control over their functions (having autonomy). Just as you analyzed your management *style* earlier in the chapter, your function as a manager must involve constant review—of yourself. In a sense, the new ways seem a mirror image of the old. Instead of a manager constantly questioning an employee about the job function, that manager must constantly question himself or herself.

The following questions are only a partial list of the behavior you should monitor in yourself. As you get more and more involved in the process (and the success) of formal organization planning, you will add to the list yourself. (We also refer you to Back-to-Basics Management as a splendid resource for do-it-yourself management techniques.)

- Do I ask employees to participate and contribute so that they can shape their own work, or do I use their ideas myself?
- Do I give them a chance to change or modify their objectives/goals?
- Do I ask them for ideas about the total department/company?
- Do I "stay off their backs" and not hover over them, allowing them to organize their own work?
- Do I let them seek help when they need it and not volunteer to "take over" when they get into trouble?
- Can they judge when their work is completed, or do they have to wait for me to say so?
- Do I ask them to voluntarily point out "pitfalls" when they see them, so we can work together on them in advance?
- Do I have an "open door" to informal communication, or am I "too busy"?

TIPS FOR MANAGERS WITH PROBLEMS

James F. Evered, in his book *Shirt-Sleeves Management*, provides a series of lists of hard-nosed tips for managers who find themselves in certain problem situations. These tips are compatible with the MBO process and fit in very nicely with the managers' plans for alternative actions when the unexpected occurs or when the back-to-basics organization/personnel plan needs modification to adapt to changing situations. Perhaps you will find them helpful.

High Employee Turnover
1. "Plan ahead for human resources needs" (fundamental to MBO).
2. "Match job/people specifications" (ditto).
3. "Select above-average people" (the need for criteria is obvious).
4. "Train people thoroughly" (back to Chapter 1).
5. "Provide continuous coaching and ongoing training" (ditto).
6. "Provide full-spectrum management of people" (involvement, participation, autonomy).
7. "Keep employees fully informed at all times" (communication—Chapter 1).

Lack of in-job growth
1. "Provide challenging opportunities" (temporary assignments, task forces).
2. "Recognize achievement" (the payoff).
3. "Delegate to the maximum." (Yes!)
4. "Provide training for growth." (Are you listening?)
5. "Give constant encouragement" (feedback, reward).
6. "Maintain high expectations" (and satisfy them).
7. "Develop 'stretching' goals" (the first approach to implementing MBO).

Goals not being met
1. "Encourage employee participation in goal setting" (fundamental).
2. "Give necessary training and coaching." (Got it?)
3. "Solicit employee suggestions." (This is the heart of the process.)
4. "Give plenty of feedback" (as we said).
5. "Provide positive reinforcement" (as opposed to management by terror).
6. "Keep all goals realistic" (and attainable).
7. "Set a personal example" (don't expect more of others than you're willing to give/do yourself).

Possible union organization
(The following criteria should apply in all business relationships.)
1. "Provide good working conditions."
2. "Provide adequate income."
3. "Listen to employees and respond to them."
4. "Maintain an open-door policy."
5. "Provide in-job growth."
6. "Treat people as valuable human beings."

Manager's job overloaded
(With proper back-to-basics organization planning, the following reminders will at least be a part of your plan; they may even be unnecessary because they have become a part of your very fiber.)
1. Select above-average people.
2. Train all employees.
3. Delegate to the maximum.
4. Maintain high expectations.
5. Recognize achievement.
6. Allow maximum free rein.
7. Use participative management.
8. Display trust and faith in people.

THE HUMAN FACTOR
IN ORGANIZATION PLANNING

It should be obvious by now that the fundamental thrust of good, back-to-basics organization planning emphasizes the *human factor*. In the last half of the twentieth century, most of the seminal writing, much of the reorganization of companies and many of the touted success stories have concentrated on human wants and needs, human satisfaction, for in that realm the ultimate success of the business can be assured.

The leading writers in the field include Maslow, Herzberg, McClelland, Argyris, McGregor, Likert, Blake and others. We recommend them to your attention. They have dealt with the human being's fundamental needs, or *"maintenance factors,"* and with the *motivators*, or "achievement factors." Figure 5.6 illustrates the hierarchy of human wants and needs and how they pay off for the company or employer.

Figure 5.6
The Hierarchy of
Human Wants and Needs

It should be obvious that these needs operate on the personal as well as the business level and that enlightened managements prosper when they create an environment and process in which these needs can be respected and satisfied.

Translating Human Wants and Needs into Management Procedures

There is no mystery to translating employee wants and needs into management functions. It is an orderly process, summarized in Figure 5.7. From the figure, it is apparent that specific *policies* and *procedures* can be created based on the requirements of the manager and the employees. *Monitoring* employee performance may then be done with the following steps:

1. List key job duties.
2. Agree upon expected results.

3.   Decide what to measure.
4.   Decide how to measure.
5.   Discuss and record achievement.
6.   Establish improvement objectives.
7.   Start the process over again.

Figure 5.7
Translating Employee Needs
into Management Functions

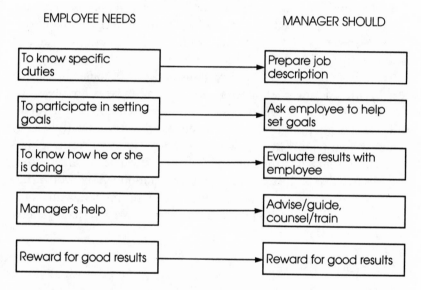

Before we go into the technicalities of developing personnel policies and procedures and a back-to-basics personnel plan, we would like to share a personal credo about this process: *An individual's personal objectives and life goals must somehow relate to the organization's goals and standards. Personal values cannot be in conflict with company values.*

This is important to remember as an employee, as a manager, as the president/owner of a company. No explanation is required; the reasons are self-evident, both from a personal point of view and from a company point of view.

THE BACK-TO-BASICS ORGANIZATION PLANNING PROCESS

As we have stated, many books have been written on the organization-planning process, and it would be unseemly to try to cover all that material in one chapter. We have given you the foregoing summary to introduce you to the philosophy of organization planning, and what follows is an overview of the steps you will follow in its implementation.

One further word about implementing a new process: Don't be afraid to use a consultant. Although times change, and sometimes consultants are looked upon as a waste or an unnecessary addition to the process, they can make significant contributions in areas such as this. They have years of experience in the organization-planning process as well as its pitfalls and can become that good "right arm" during the analysis and preparation work involved in instituting a new methodology. The good consultants will involve all your people from the beginning and work together with you to make it your plan. This is a prime example of "not reinventing the wheel." Ultimately, the time and money saved on research, the pitfalls avoided and the speed of implementation will be worth the cost and effort of using a consultant. If done properly, all your employees will make the plan their own and have a vested interest in making it work.

The Planning Steps

1. Define the work to be done, the tasks, the departments. (You might find yourself reorganizing your company when you define the work by tasks rather than by people).
    Define the skills to do each job.
    Define the time to do each job.
    This defines the human factor—the people to do the work (types, training, number).
2. Write the job description. Extensive guidelines have been published on what job descriptions are, what they should include, how they should be evaluated and how they should relate to each other. Writing the job description is initially the work of manager *and* employee. Evaluation could use outside help. Defining relationships requires much

management time and input.

3. Employee and manager set work goals, develop action plans and agree on the method and time frame for their implementation.

4. Set up a process, both written and in person, for the orderly review of these work goals. Recent studies indicate that performance reviews are more beneficial if they are performed more than once a year and if they are *not* necessarily related to merit increases, bonuses, etc.

5. Set up an orderly and companywide training and guidance program. This can range from training the secretarial staff in word-processing equipment to initiating support of continuing education in job-related and/or stretching programs. Training and guidance keep your employees on the cutting edge of change, not running behind the rest of the pack.

6. Establish salary grade levels, promotion flexibility, transfer flexibility, promotion incentives and salary-increase incentives that are competitive within your own industry and with related industries.

7. Create an orderly review process for your job descriptions, salary grade levels, promotion and salary increase guidelines so that *you* know you maintain a competitive edge.

8. Set up procedures for reviewing not only progress but problems and set up universal and equitable guidelines for dealing with problem people; this means itemizing, in detailed personnel policies and procedures, the methods you wish *your* managers to use, and to use consistently and equitably.

9. Reward your employees consistently and fairly for work well done. Set up additional incentive rewards for the superachievers. These can range from family vacations for the supersalesperson and incentive bonuses for surpassing a goal to restricted stock plans and company ownership awards.

The Personnel Plan

The personnel plan is a fundamental part of the process of preparing your back-to-basics plan. The organization planning that we have reviewed is the bedrock on which your personnel plan is built, but now you must concern yourself more with numbers than with processes. Those numbers will be derived from all the work you have previously done. The following are the steps in the process of personnel analysis by which you prepare your personnel plan:

1. Identify the resources of the company (what are the sales projections, what is your expected profit margin, etc.?).
    What are your expected revenues?
    What are your fixed costs (other than people)? (See the chapter on quantifying.)
    What are the department's/company's required profits (or acceptable losses)?
    What are your relative costs (not people-related costs, but those costs related to production)?

2. Analyze your people costs.
    List the number and kinds of jobs. (See the "Head Count" page of the back-to-basics plan as a guideline.) Can you use more or less people, different kinds of people, based on the needs indicated in your business plan?
    Analyze your union requirements. Can you cut, or must you expand? When is the next contract up for renewal? How do you expect it to go?
    Are your salaries competitive? Will you have turnover? Do you overpay?
    Build in incentives for overachievers.

These exercises will prepare you to fill out the financial and personnel sections of your back-to-basics business plan. Remember one word as you embark on the process of back-to-basics planning: *justification*. If you have trouble justifying all the requests in that plan, perhaps you should take another good, hard look at it before you pass it along to upper management. If you *can* justify the requests, then you have done your management job well, and both your staff and your superiors will be happy with you.

CHECKLIST FOR THE ORGANIZATION PLAN
"Form follows function."

The development of an organization that best serves the tasks to be performed is the primary objective in organization planning. The best back-to-basics planners/managers strive for flexibility, autonomy and participation among all employees in the organization. Here are some reminders on how to achieve those goals:

- Most American businesses are organized like the military. Your objective should be to tap all that human potential, not draw little boxes on an organization chart.
- "Quality circles" allocate human resources by task, not by department. Problem solving in that kind of environment involves utilizing many skills from many sources. The whole is often stronger than the sum of its parts.
- Flexibility in an organization, the ability to function effectively in a changing world, is a good beginning for management by objectives.
- Since "form follows function," tasks should dictate the type of people and their mode of interrelationship in an enterprise.
- Management by objective fundamentally involves the management of people.
- MBO defines the goals and the methods of reaching them and establishes qualitative measurement of the progress toward achieving them.
- MBO can be instituted in three ways:
    Set objectives above what is currently done.
    Incorporate personnel goals with corporate goals on an annual basis.
    Integrate MBO into your long-range strategic planning.
- Everyone manages something: people, money, resources, assets, departments.
- Analyze your management style: Are you "X" or "Y"? Do you direct or delegate?
- MBO can be threatening to people who do not welcome responsibility for their own actions.

- Why use MBO?
  It allows the greatest flexibility in managing people.
  It enables a manager to manage and permits all employees to feel themselves a part of the process.
  Therefore, everyone plays a meaningful role in the enterprise.
  With everyone a part of the process, all are dedicated to achieving a venture's goals.
- The future is now. How will we work in the last quarter of the twentieth century?
  We work in teams, interdependently.
  We must learn to manage changing life-styles.
  There are more large-scale enterprises—conglomerates.
  We are a young working nation (50 percent of the work force is under 30) and there are more workers over 65. This demographic change alters a whole range of key business factors, from benefits to marketing.
  We are a more educated society, seeking more challenges.
  People seek greater involvement, participation and autonomy in their work.
- Other people can slow you down, as the "doubting Thomases" look for reasons not to fully implement your MBO program.
- Avoid the pitfalls:
  Check the progress of your plan on a regular basis.
  Define the problems and analyze their source.
  Look at your options; what can you change?
  Initiate an alternate plan to bring others aboard.
- Avoid superficial and nonconnected programs. Programs must make sense to all and have a payoff to be effective.
- Your personnel policies and procedures provide the payoff for your back-to-basics organization plan.
- What are the functions of management under MBO?
  Planning
  Organizing
  Performing
  Controlling
  Reviewing
- Managing people is like managing a company: Process and

purpose are interconnected.

- Instead of managers constantly questioning employees, managers should also question themselves.
- Whether your problem as a manager is high employee turnover, lack of in-job growth, unmet goals or management overload, the one universally applicable solution is *training* your employees.
- Take fundamental human needs and motivators into account in designing your MBO plan. Once the physical, safety and social needs are fulfilled, employees want more: They want self-esteem and, ultimately, self-actualization (a maximization of their ability and potential).
- Translate employee needs into management functions:

   Prepare job descriptions so employees will know their duties.

   Ask employees to help set goals.

   Evaluate results so employees will know how they're doing.

   Advise, guide, counsel and train to supply the help employees need.

   Reward for good results.

- Monitor the performance of your employees by:

   Identifying key job duties.

   Indicating the expected results.

   Identifying which results to measure.

   Determining ways of measuring the results.

   Measuring achievement at prescribed times.

   Rewarding for good results.

   Listing areas to be improved.

   Starting the monitoring process over again.

- An individual's personal objectives and life goals must somehow relate to the organization's goals and standards. Personal values cannot be in conflict with company values.
- Don't be afraid to use consultants to help implement MBO; maybe you can avoid "reinventing the wheel."
- The steps for personnel planning are:

   Define the work to be done in terms of skill, time and number of people.

   Identify company resources: revenues, costs, expected profits.

Analyze your people costs in terms of number and kinds of jobs, competitive rates, benefits packages and incentives.

Write the job descriptions.

Set work goals, action plans and a time-frame.

Establish a review process.

Set up training and guidance programs.

Establish salary/grade levels with review and increase guidelines.

Devise a review process for reviewing the success of your own back-to-basics planning and management, so that you stay competitive.

Develop guidelines for problems and problem people.

Set up equitable payoffs and incentives.

- Always remember the word *justification* when preparing a personnel plan.

6 QUANTIFYING

"A good budget means never having to say 'no.'"

A friend tells the story of a doctor she knew who had trouble with his car. He took it to his mechanic, told him some of the symptoms, then asked what the mechanic thought might be wrong. The mechanic said, "Well, you know, a million things could be wrong. You have to get inside and take a look and test things and explore all the possibilities before you know for sure. It could be related to a lot of things. You know, doctor, my job is a lot like yours."

The doctor thought for a couple of seconds and then replied, "Yes, but I have to fix it while it's still running."

And that's probably the best definition of a back-to-basics business manager, financial manager and budget planner. We have to fix things while they're still running. (If we've planned well, perhaps they won't need "fixing," but turnabouts can occur.)

Letting the engine stop is not really one of the preferred options in developing a good financial plan. If the financial "engine" ever does stop, it could be pretty hard to get it going again.

Simply put, back-to-basics financial planning derives from a sound budgeting process—a budgeting process that begins by talking with people. And that must be honest talk, based on mutual respect and mutual understanding.

RESPECT AND UNDERSTANDING

To have respect and understanding, the back-to-basics financial person must be schooled in, must be familiar with, what the other manager does—not just in the intellectual sense, not just in terms of knowledge gained from reading a job description, but from observing and listening. If necessary, the financial person should sit in the unit or department for several days to learn what people really do. From that understanding will come the respect necessary to help translate that doing, that activity, that work, into a meaningful budget (and other necessary financial documents) for inclusion in a back-to-basics business plan. And people who are not in financial departments need to go through a similar exercise.

How many times have you heard the businesspeople in your organization referred to as "bean counters"? It is derogatory at best and indicates a lack of understanding and respect for the business of business.

Mutual understanding and respect—these are the two legs of the stool that supports sound financial planning. The third leg, of course, is communication: the willingness—indeed, the eagerness—to talk, to share, to develop ideas together (as we have discussed in earlier chapters).

ESTABLISHING CONTROL BY SAYING YES

Budgets exist to control money. And budgeting control begins with:

- An understanding of the organization, the way it does business, its goals, its image, its needs.
- An understanding of the problems of each of the areas (we're

back to talking with people).

- An understanding of the individuals involved in the process.

How do you control costs? More often than not, by saying yes. You control costs by providing alternatives for the way people have suggested doing something. And in essence, you're saying yes to the problems they are trying to solve. (Remember, if you do have to say no, say it diplomatically, apologetically and with enormous concern.)

If you can build up rapport, if you can establish the fact that you understand other people's business, if you can find ways to help solve problems, *if you can say yes a lot*—then people will listen to you when you truly need to say no (when there *are* no other alternatives).

Sound business practices are vital, whether your venture is profit or nonprofit, industrial or artistic; but it is likely that control—total ,control—of ventures, should not be based on financial decisions (or be made by financial people). In the best of all worlds, and the best of all planning, decisions are an outgrowth of a partnership, where vision and planning for the future combine with the disciplines of finance.

WHO NEEDS FINANCIAL REPORTS?

This chapter deals with some financial reports that make planning and management possible. It is not our intention to teach accounting or finance; rather, the material is intended as a summary, for the "nonfinancial manager," of those monetary concepts that are fundamental to a complete, comprehensive, cooperative plan.

Remember two things: You have to start with an understanding of the company, the people, their problems; and control of the numbers gives you more opportunity to say yes.

Owners, manager, suppliers, credit grantors and others in a business enterprise are confronted with financial statements. Although these statements generally seem to proliferate, become more detailed—and occasionally, more confusing—as the enterprise grows or gets more complex, it is advantageous (for the nonfinancial manager, particularly) to remember that the purpose of these financial statements is really very simple and direct. They exist to:

Record accurately the financial activities of the enterprise.

Measure that financial activity against the past.

Project financial activity in the future based on current knowledge.

That's all. And in all candor, the only type of financial statement required by law is the first: the type that records accurately the financial activity of the enterprise. Stockholders, the SEC, the IRS and all the other interested outside parties are entitled to complete, accurate, honest records.

The measurement and projection statements can truly be regarded as management tools (not financial reports), useful in helping the enterprise keep track of the details of its operation and thereby be as successful as possible.

Remember Mayor Ed Koch's famous question, "How'm I doing?" Every manager should ask the question, "How are we doing?" Financial records should exist to answer that question. They should *not* exist to decorate office bookshelves or fill up computer bins.

The Operating Budget (Figure 6.1) is a *worksheet* for preparing your cost projections for the planning period. While its use is undoubtedly self-evident at a glance, a few comments might be in order.

The increases (or decreases) under the section called "Next Year" allow you to break out the economic assumptions which management has given to you from the individual assumptions which are peculiarly your own. In other words, this worksheet relates directly to the Assumptions page (Figure 7.1) of your planning package. It allows you to calculate the "knowns" for all your general ledger items, before you start dealing with the "unknowns" (New Projects, Alternate Plans, etc.).

It also allows you to make a "first cut" at the quarterly expenses before you prepare your Summary form (Figure 7.5).

This form is *not* for management; it is a preliminary working tool for you. However, it *can* come in handy as a back-up reference when you're asked the question, "Why did this item go up so much on next year's plan?"

Figure 6.1
Operating Budget

19___ PLAN

Dept. name: _____   Prepared by: _____

Dept. number: _____   Date prepared: _____

GL No.	General Ledger Description	Latest Estimate This Year	Salary Increases	Production Increases	Inflation Assumption	Overhead Increases	Other Increases	Total	1st Qtr.	2d Qtr.	3d Qtr.	4th Qtr.

Next Year

You must avoid the trap of unread data, unclear data, too much data, nonuseful data. If a financial report arrives on the desk of a manager who does not want to read it immediately, one of three things is probably wrong:

- The data aren't useful for managing that segment of the business and should be reviewed with an eye to possible revamping.
- The manager hasn't been trained properly in the use of the data for the managerial process.
- You've got the wrong manager in the job.

Now that we know that financial reports exist for only three reasons (to *record* the firm's financial activities, *measure* those activities against the past and *project* those activities in the future), we can ask, "What material should be on them?" Again, the answer is much simpler than the plethora of financial statements in an enterprise would suggest. Financial reports contain information on the following topics:

Revenue	Company assets
Costs	Company liabilities
Profits or losses	

That's all. Everything else that may come to mind—sales analyses, departmental budgets, product mix or production costs, market trends and share of dollars, unit costs, pricing comparisons—is *details* of doing business, not the simple financial reports required. These other statements are the *embellishments* of the above broad categories. They aid management in analyzing its position among its competition and preparing its strategies for the future; they are *not* pure financial data.

In the remainder of this chapter, you will see examples and simple explanations of some of the principal financial reporting forms, which—in their many variations—are used by most companies. The intent is to familiarize you with the formats, the formulas, the definitions and the purpose of the basic reports. Variations on these forms would be based on the purposes and needs of your own company. Let's take out the jargon and get back to basics.

TWO BASIC CONCEPTS:
REVENUES AND COSTS

Revenues and costs are the two fundamental concepts in running an enterprise and creating financial reports.

Revenues

The term *revenues* refers to all the income an enterprise generates. The firm may sell products, services, theater tickets or time sharing on a computer, or it may share another company's income as a commission. But the heading "revenues" on a financial statement refers to all the income generated by the enterprise during a particular time frame (weekly, monthly, quarterly, annually).

The degree of detail included on the financial report is generally at the discretion of the company, but basically, the primary source of income (main business of the company) and subsidiary income follow in order of importance (see Figures 6.2 and 6.3).

Figure 6.2
Example: Calculation of Total Gross Revenues

Gross revenues
    Sales (product line) $
    Merchandising (co-op, etc.)
    Publication sales (ads, books)
    Other   _____
        TOTAL $_____

Figure 6.3
Example: Calculation of Total Gross Revenues

Gross revenues
    Ticket Sales $
    Concessions
    Program ads
    Other (parking, etc.)   _____
        TOTAL $_____

Many financial reports require an adjustment to the gross revenues to accurately reflect the operation of the business. For example, products may be discounted for merchandising purposes or for special distribution, theater tickets may be discounted for group sales or subscription, or advertising revenues may be discounted for agency commission. The revenue section of the financial report should indicate such adjustments (see Figure 7.4).

Costs

Costs are incurred by all enterprises. The nature and importance of costs will vary from business to business. For instance, telephone costs would be larger and more important in a sales solicitation company than in an accounting firm. But putting costs in the appropriate category is a major part of the exercise.

Figure 6.4
Example: Calculation of Total Net Revenues

Gross revenues
    Sales $
    Merchandising
    Publication sales
    Other   _____
       TOTAL $_____

Adjustments
    Sales commission $
    Distribution costs
    Other discounts
       TOTAL   − $_____
        TOTAL NET REVENUES $_____

Costs are generally divided into two categories: fixed and variable:

- *Fixed costs* are generally assumed to be those costs that remain constant (within a given fiscal time frame) no matter how well or badly the company is doing. Examples are rent, taxes, utilities, insurance, depreciation and salaries of key executives.

- *Variable costs* are those expenses that generally rise or fall based on business activity, particularly in the manufacturing and service sectors. They include such items as labor costs, material for production, advertising expenses, employee commissions, promotional expenses, travel and entertainment, supplies and office expenses.

Managers will also use the phrases *controllable costs* and *noncontrollable costs*. Don't fall into the trap of believing that they are the same as *variable costs* and *fixed costs*. The latter are legitimate accounting terms that aid in the separation of expenses requiring different accounting treatment (depreciation of office equipment versus expensing of travel tickets bought in advance, for instance). However, *controllable* and *noncontrollable* are *managerial* terms, *not* accounting terms. They signify expense areas where managerial decision making can alter the cost of running a business. (The decision to sublet office space, for instance, thereby reducing the overall rent bill; firing executives to reduce the real and accompanying overhead; changing the insurance payment method to alter cash flow and increase income—these are all *management* decisions that can alter the nature of a fixed cost by making it "controllable" or "noncontrollable.")

Got it? (Don't worry; the whole subject and methodology of cost control are a topic unto themselves.)

Although the appearance of the expense section of the financial report can be as varied as the creative genius of your resident accountant, it is obvious from the above that there are two main options. Expenses can be shown in terms of:

Manufacturing and operating costs (see Figure 6.5).
Fixed and variable costs (see Figure 6.6).

Figure 6.5
Example: Expenses Shown in Terms of
Manufacturing and Operating Costs

Total net revenues $_____

Manufacturing costs
   Cost of goods sold $
   Material
   Direct labor
   Manufacturing overhead   _____
     Total   – $_____
Gross profit $_____

Operating costs
   Research and development $
   Sales and marketing
   General and administrative
   Allocated/financial   _____
     Total   – $_____
Profit before taxes $_____

Taxes
   Federal income tax $
   State taxes
   Local taxes   _____
     Total   – $_____
       Net Profit $_____

Figure 6.6
Example: Expenses Shown in Terms of
Fixed and Variable Costs

Total net revenues $_____

Variable costs
   Product costs
      Material $
      Labor
      Overhead
   Period costs
      Commissions
      Other   _____
        TOTAL   − $_____

Contribution to profit _____%

Fixed costs
      Fixed overhead $
      General and administrative
      Sales and marketing
      Allocated/financial   _____
        TOTAL   − $_____

Profit before taxes $_____

Taxes
      Federal income tax $
      State taxes
      Local taxes   _____
        TOTAL   − $_____
         NET PROFIT $_____

PROFIT

Now we come to the nicest word in the business dictionary—*profit*. In the 1970s it was a word that fell into disrepute along with the reputations of American business and businesspeople. While this book neither brags about nor knocks the reputation of American business, we think it must be stated that a lot of good people in honest companies took a bad rap in those glory days of the gurus. While there is much about American business practices that is dreadful, there is much that was, and is, the hope of the world. American business is the giant engine that makes this country and its people the best fed, best clothed, best housed, best informed in the history of the world. Nobody says we are perfect. We just say we top the competition. And amazingly enough, we've done it with a polyglot, not homogeneous, population. If history were our guide, we should be at war amongst ourselves instead of working together as a nation to better our own lives and those of our families.

Winston Churchill once said that democracy was the messiest, most difficult form of government in the world—until you consider the alternatives. The same might be said of the free-enterprise system—until you consider the alternatives.

So let's hear it for profits! While they motivate some to venal, greedy behavior, for others they represent a joyous, exciting opportunity to improve our futures. Pearl Bailey is said to have once commented, "I've been rich and I've been poor. Rich is better." The bottom line, in any enterprise: Profits are better.

Happily, college students today seem to be returning to the idea that a career in business is a valuable, worthwhile endeavor, and they are buckling down to study and are preparing themselves for a place in the free-enterprise system. One of us tells the students at the Yale School of Drama who are studying to be arts administrators: "Don't let the words *not for profit* fool you. *Someone* had to have made a profit so that you can run a theater at a deficit. So be damn sure you run it at a *low* deficit, with high quality and with integrity. The people who worked so hard for the original profit deserve at least that."

Profits (or losses) can be reported as straight numerical figures, as in the previous examples.   But often, to gain management attention, the reporting of these figures is made more dramatic by the use of percentages, bar charts or line graphs (see Figures 6.7 and 6.8). Remember, such techniques are purely an enhancement of

Figure 6.7
Bar Charts Showing Profits and Losses

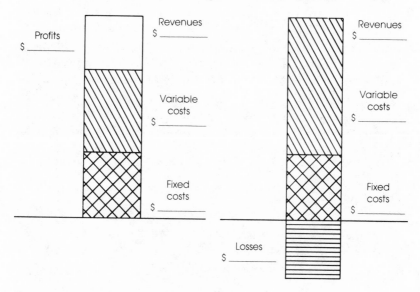

Figure 6.8
Line Graphs Showing Profits and Losses

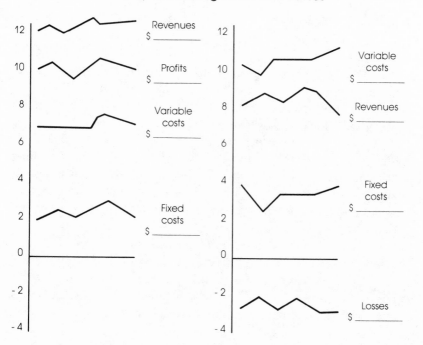

the actual numerical data to give management a quick graphic response to that question we posed earlier—"How are we doing?"

You will often hear the phrases *return on investment* and *return on equity*, which are a businesslike way (particularly attractive to Wall Street analysts of publicly held companies) of evaluating a venture's progress. These phrases refer to statistical measurements of the financial progress of a firm. One of the most graphic and helpful examples of the exercise required to arrive at these numbers that we have ever seen was developed by Ann Gray, then treasurer of the American Broadcasting Companies, Inc. We include it for your use (see Figure 6.9).

BALANCE SHEET

A business is always in a condition of equity; i.e., what it owns equals what it owes, either to its creditors or to its owners. This can be expressed in equation form as follows:

$$\text{Assets} = \text{Liabilities} + \text{Owners' Equity}$$

Assets = resources that the business owns.

Liabilities = obligations owed by the business to persons or businesses other than its owners.

Owners' equity = what the business owes the owners.

The balance sheet shows all of these items on the last day of the accounting period (which is usually a calendar year).

For purposes of analysis (and to facilitate use of the examples presented), further classification is considered necessary.

Some *assets* are of greater utility than others. Financial analysts recognize this greater utility, and a special category of assets called "current assets" has been established. Current assets consist of cash and other assets that can reasonably be expected to be converted to cash or sold or consumed in the near future in the course of the normal operations of the business.

Usually, the next category of assets is "plant assets," or "fixed assets." They are expected to last a relatively long time (more than one year); are fixed in size, shape or form; and are used by the business in its operation. The fact that the life of the assets extends over several fiscal periods makes it necessary to allocate the cost

Figure 6.9
Calculation of Return on Investment

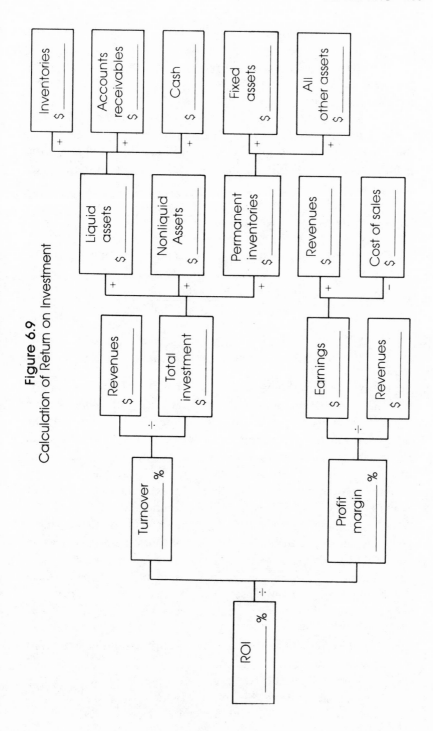

over several fiscal periods. This allocation is called depreciation accounting.

The last category of assets is usually called "other" and includes any items that do not reasonably fit into the first two categories, such as stocks, bonds, patents and copyrights.

Liabilities usually fall into the categories of "current" and "long-term." Current liabilities cover the obligations owed to creditors, that must be paid within the current fiscal period. Long-term liabilities are those liabilities that are not to be paid in the current fiscal period.

Stockholders' equity, or owners' equity, occupies the third section of the balance sheet and includes what the business owes to its owners.

There are two ways to analyze a company's balance sheet:

1. $\text{Current ratio} = \dfrac{\text{current assets}}{\text{current liabilities}}$

2. $\text{Working capital} = \text{current assets} - \text{current liabilities}$

Both formulas help the back-to-basics financial planner to measure a company's financial strength. They help in evaluating a company's ability to pay its obligations. Please remember that the ratios that measure the strength of a company (a ratio of over 1.00, for instance) will vary from one type of business to another. One business might be very cash-oriented, while another might be heavily equipment-oriented. Their ratios would vary, but they could both be very healthy companies financially.

The balance sheet is not especially useful for management purposes in its traditional form (see Figure 6.10). Changes in business activity that affect elements of the balance sheet are not clearly shown. As with the income statement, the balance sheet can be modified to be more useful to management (see Figure 6.11). The elements can be grouped into three major categories:

- Working capital (with a minor adjustment to correct any short-term debt).
- Property, plant and equipment, together with other assets.
- Capital structure of the business (which would include other liabilities, long-term debt and shareholders' equity).

The American Management Associations presents an interesting view as a management tool:

Working capital is traditionally defined as current assets minus current liabilities. We would like to slightly modify this definition and eliminate short-term debt. This way *all* debt can be considered part of the financial resources of the business. Working capital would include such things as cash, accounts receivable, inventories, prepaid expenses, accounts payable, accrued expenses, and accrued taxes.

What happens to accounts receivable if sales increase? Obviously, if a company sells on credit and the terms and conditions of the sale are established, if sales increase, it can be expected that accounts receivable would also increase, probably proportionately. Similarly, what happens to inventory? If sales go up, then the costs associated with producing those sales (that is, the variable costs of the goods manufactured) will go up. If the variable costs of the goods manufactured increase, inventories can be expected to increase to accommodate the higher levels of product being sold. Because there may be some diseconomies of scale in the inventory area, these costs may not increase absolutely proportionately, but it is fair to assume that they will increase relatively proportionately. What happens to accounts payable? If the inventories go up, it would suggest that the firm is buying more materials to produce the product and, as a result, accounts payable will also increase. What happens to accrued expenses? Accrued expenses generally represent wages and salaries not paid at the end of an accounting period. If the level of activity increases, the number of employees is also probably increasing, as is the level of accrued expenses. In essence, increases in sales activity result in increases in virtually all of the working capital accounts. Most businesses' current assets exceed their current liability, that is, they have positive working capital. It can also be said that if a business increases its sales level, the demands on it for increased working capital are greater. Most managers understand this, but may not fully appreciate it in the context of their company's financial statements.

What is interesting about working capital is that it behaves in a fashion similar to variable costs. As sales increase, working capital increases. As sales decrease, working capital should decrease.

What about the lower left hand part of the revised balance sheet, the property, plant, and equipment and other assets? Will they necessarily increase with increases in sales? Will more land be bought? Will the plant be expanded proportionately with increases in sales? Will equipment be purchased proportionately with

Figure 6.10
Traditional Balance Sheet

ASSETS

Current assets
  Cash $
  Accounts
  receivable
  Inventory
  Prepaid
  expenses   _____
  TOTAL $_____

Property, plant and
equipment
  Land $_____
  Buildings
  Equipment   _____
  Accumulated
  depreciation _____
  TOTAL $_____

Other assets
  Investments $
  Patents
  Organization
  expense   _____
  TOTAL $_____
TOTAL ASSETS $_____

LIABILITIES AND EQUITY

Current liabilities
  Accounts
  payable $
  Notes payable
  Accrued
  expenses
  Accrued taxes _____
  TOTAL $_____

Other liabilities $_____
Long-term debt
  Notes payable— $
  bank
  Mortgage
  payable   _____
  TOTAL $_____

Shareholders' equity
  Paid-in capital $
  Retained
  earnings   _____
  TOTAL $_____
TOTAL LIABILITIES
AND EQUITY $_____

increases in sales? Will these things happen automatically? Probably not. The acquisition of property, plant, and equipment in most businesses normally goes through some form of an appropriation and authorization cycle and, at this time, the need for additional fixed assets is evaluated. When fixed assets are added, they are frequently added in large units. In many respects, fixed assets act like fixed costs. Fixed assets do not increase directly and proportionately with increases in sales activity, but normally go up in a step-like function over reasonable ranges of activity. They do not increase automatically and are usually affected by managerial decisions.

Working capital, fixed assets, and other assets may be thought of as the assets employed by a business. Think of the manager's job in terms of the return generated on the assets employed, where return is

Figure 6.11
Modified Balance Sheet

> _Working Capital_
> Current assets minus current liabilities

> _Property, Plant and
> Equipment, Plus Other
> Assets_

> _Capital Structure
> of the Business_
> Other liabilities
> Long-term debt
> Shareholders' equity

measured by the profits or income of the business, and the assets employed are measured by the working capital, fixed assets, and other assets. Improved performance is represented by increased return on assets employed; increased return on assets employed may be accomplished by increasing profits while holding the assets employed in the business constant, or a combination of the two. It is the manager's job to use assets as effectively as possible to generate profits.

How have the assets employed in the business been financed? That question takes us to the third major section of the modified balance sheet—the _capital structure._ We will define capital structure to include all of the debt, whether it be short-term or long-term, and the shareholders' equity. Equity includes both paid-in capital from investors plus earnings retained into the business. Obviously, if a business wants to grow it will require additional working capital and perhaps additional fixed assets and other assets. The net income that is generated in many businesses is inadequate to finance these additional investments. As a result, businesses require new capital, either debt or equity, for them to realize their desired growth.

Assume for a moment that a business does not use any debt financing and that it has a 15 percent return on assets employed. In this case, its return on capital structure, consisting entirely of equity, would similarly be 15 percent. However, should the firm finance its business by a combination of debt and equity, a higher return on equity would be generated to its shareholders. This use of debt financing to generate a higher return to equity investors is known as *financial leverage*. Financial leverage is prudent to a point. Excessive debt runs the risk of not being payable out of the firm's ongoing cash flows and, as a result, can put the business into bankruptcy.

This view of the balance sheet consisting of working capital, fixed assets, other assets, and capital structure is useful because it connects the relationship between changes in operations reflected in the income statement and the effect of those changes on various parts of the balance sheet. The manager who understands these relationships will be able to make better decisions in the context of the total business.[1]

THE FUNDS-FLOW STATEMENT

Another financial statement commonly used in business planning is called the "funds-flow statement," "sources and uses of funds," or "statement of change in financial position." This statement shows the movement of funds through a business over time. The traditional format is depicted in Figure 6.12, where all the sources of funds are accumulated (including those from the operations of the business, new sources of capital such as debt and equity, and the sale of fixed assets), and all the uses of funds are likewise accumulated (such as the purchase of fixed assets), the repayment of debt and the distribution of dividends). The bottom line is the net change in working capital; hence, when you think of funds, you may conclude that funds mean working capital. Supplementary detailed schedules of the changes in working capital are normally provided. This traditional form may satisfy the accounting profession, but managerially, it is not terribly useful.

If we make some adjustments, as we did with the balance sheet, we can present a format more useful to the manager (see Figure 6.13). We can start the modified funds-flow statement in the same fashion as the traditional one; that is, accumulate the funds accruing from the operations of the business. As a business grows, it may require increases in working capital, and such increases can be

---

1. Quoted by permission of the American Management Associations.

Figure 6.12
Traditional Uses of Funds Statement

SOURCES OF FUNDS

Net income plus depreciation $_____
Funds from operations $
Debt financing
Equity financing   _____
    TOTAL SOURCES $_____

USES OF FUNDS

   Debt repayment $
   Capital investments
   Dividends   _____
      TOTAL USES   — $_____
        NET CHANGE IN WORKING
        CAPITAL $_____

called an operating flow of the business. Increases in business activity may prompt the acquisition of new fixed assets. We can therefore think of the operating flow of the business (the funds generated through the income statement) as being partially offset by additional investments in working capital, fixed assets and other assets.

We must also be aware of immediate and long-term financing needs, as they are offset by the dividend obligation to shareholders (as demonstrated in the bottom section of Figure 6.12).

Restructuring your cash flow in this way allows you to analyze cash availability for operations as well as for long-term financing. Also, by calculating your operating funds and your financing funds (using this method) as a percent of sales, you can determine whether your current profit margin (profit as a percent of sales) is healthy enough to sustain your financing plans or operating plans. Put another way, is your profit margin higher or lower than your operating funds percent-to-sales or your financing funds percent-to-sales?

Figure 6.13
Modified Uses of Funds Statement

OPERATING FUNDS USAGE

Net income plus depreciation $_____
    Funds from Operations
    Investment in Working Capital
    Investment in Fixed Assets   _____
        OPERATING FUNDS $_____

FINANCIAL FUNDS USAGE

    Debt Financing/(Repayments)
    Equity Financing
    less: Dividends   _____
        FINANCING FUNDS $_____

Figure 6.14
Proforma Department Expense Budget

	Jan.	Feb.	March	April	May	June	July	Aug.	Sept.	Oct.	Nov.	Dec.	Total
Wages and salaries													
Salaried													
Hourly													
Union labor													
Supervisory (manufac-turing)													
Engineering													
Sales and marketing													
General and adminis-trative													
SUBTOTAL													
Fringe Benefits													
Premium pay													
Payroll taxes													
Sickness and vaca-tion pay													
Workers' compensation													
Other													
SUBTOTAL													

	Jan.	Feb.	March	April	May	June	July	Aug.	Sept.	Oct.	Nov.	Dec.	Total
Variable overhead (manufacturing)													
Manufacturing supplies													
Repairs and maintenance													
Other													
SUBTOTAL													
Fixed overhead (manufacturing)													
Utilities													
Telephone													
Rent													
Insurance													
Amortization													
Other													
SUBTOTAL													
Engineering													
Engineering supplies													
Repairs and maintenance													
Other													
SUBTOTAL													
Sales and Marketing													
Variable													
Commissions													
Other													
SUBTOTAL													

Fixed
Travel and entertainment
Promotion and advertising
Warehousing
Other
SUBTOTAL

General and Administrative
Accounting
Consulting
Legal
Office supplies
Utilities
Telephone
Rent
Insurance
Depreciation
Amortization
Other
SUBTOTAL

Financial
Interest
Bad debts
Taxes
SUBTOTAL
TOTAL

Figure 6.15
Proforma Cash-Flow Statement (Operational)

	Jan.	Feb.	March	April	May	June	July	Aug.	Sept.	Oct.	Nov.	Dec.	Total
Cash Receipts													
Collection of accounts receivable													
Sale of assets													
Borrowings													
Equity financing													
Other													
TOTAL													
Cash expenditures													
Material													
Freight													
Wages and salaries													
Commissions													
Fringe benefits													
Manufacturing expenses													
Selling expenses													
General and administrative expenses													
Financial expenses													
SUBTOTAL													
Cash Expenditures													
Capital expenditures													
Debt repayment													
Dividends													
Other													

TOTAL
Cash Flows
CUMULATIVE
CASH
FLOWS

Figure 6.16
Proforma Financial Performance Statistics

	Jan.	Feb.	March	April	May	June	July	Aug.	Sept.	Oct.	Nov.	Dec.	Total
Sales growth (percentage year to year)													
Contribution (percentage of net sales)													
Net income (percentage of net sales)													
Working capital (percentage of net sales)													
Accounts receivable (days outstanding)													
Inventory turnover (X)													
Net income (percentage of assets employed)													
Debt (percentage of total capital)													
Dividends (percentage of net income)													
Operating funds flows ($)													
Cash flows ($)													

KEY STATISTICS

Every company collects data on a vast range of its business activity that can be manipulated (in the best sense of that word) statistically to provide measurement tools for decision making.

These statistics can deal with unit production costs, pricing policies, employee productivity, customer acceptance trends, company problem areas, growth opportunities, keys for future marketing or future R&D—a broad range of topics of interest to an executive or manager.

Key statistics reports can be very elaborate and detailed, to the point of being nearly book-length, or they can be one-page summaries. The needs of the company will dictate the extent of the detail that is included.

However, we must confess, we have a bias. A manager's time is so precious that we feel a key statistics report that can briefly identify a broad range of information is most helpful. We're not advocating "management at a glance," but we do feel that an executive needs a tight summary of information (knowing that detailed backup is available) that can answer the questions, "Where were we?" "Where are we?" and "Where can we go?"

One of the best such reports we've ever seen was prepared by the producer of a large regional theater (see Figure 6.17). The theater had started from scratch the year before and had lost a quarter of a million dollars. This producer had been hired for the current year and had brought the losses down to $50,000 (no small feat). She had in mind certain changes for the coming year that would bring the operation to break-even or better.

It is obvious from looking at the report that she planned to emphasize subscriptions, hold down costs on the packages the theater would buy and reorganize the marketing campaign. It is a one-page summary of activity from which an entire business plan and marketing plan can be written. In our view, it is an exemplary key statistics report because it provides the raw material for questions, planning and operational decisions—all on one page.

Never forget, managers are trying to *manage*. Their jobs are hopeless if they are buried under a lot of paper. Don't let financial reports confuse you; don't let them bury you; don't let them take over your time, which is more profitably spent managing the enterprise.

Figure 6.17
Summer Theater Key Indicators

	1975 Actual	1976 Estimated	1977 Plan
Number of weeks	9	8	8
Number of seats sold	56,886	67,059	73,456
Net ticket revenue	$345,398.00	$465,792.00	$560,492.00
Price of tickets	$5.50, $6.50	$7.50, $8.50	$7.50, $8.00
	$7.50, $8.50		$8.50, $9.50
Total potential weekly *net*	$130,103.42	$150,146.88	$167,568.82
Average price of packages	$31,483.97	$37,581.25	$40,000.00
Average weekly cost	$71,102.00	$79,231.12	$76,500.00
Average weekly operating expenses	$39,992.44	$32,649.87	$36,500.00
Total advertising cost	$42, 193.00	$71,157.00	$77,000.00
Number of full subscriptions	249	1,028	1,828
Number of half-season subscriptions	—	301	300
Producers hired	1 each in March, April, June	Jan. 1976	Oct. 1976
First subscription mailing/ gift	June 1, 1975	March 5, 1976	Nov. 15, 1976
First subscription ad	June 11, 1975	April 6, 1976	Feb. 1977
Box office open (mail only)	—	April 1, 1976	Continuous
Box office open	June 20, 1975	May 12, 1976	May 1, 1977
Break-even tickets per show	10,289	9,253	9,217
Average tickets sold per show	6,321	8,382	9,182
Average price of ticket (regular season)	$6.07	$6.95	$7.63
Season capacity sold	34.02%	40.3%	43.8%
Number of passes	5,497	3,267	3,300
Number of groups sold	90	80	100
Number of group tickets sold	6,668	7,072	10,000
Total group net revenue	$28,295.36	$43,495.03	$63,000.00

However, always remember that you avoid financial data and its importance at your peril. Good managers know the details as well as the broad outlines of their operations.

Like the Greeks, we plead for the "golden mean." This brief summary of financial reports necessary for good back-to-basics planning and monitoring of a venture has been offered as an introduction to the phrases, jargon and reports with which you will deal. We do not expect that it will have made you an expert (there are scores of excellent books and courses that can give you deeper knowledge), but we do hope that it has helped familiarize you, as a "nonfinancial" manager, with the scope of information with which you must deal every day.

CHECKLIST FOR QUANTIFYING
"Good budgeting means never having to say no."

People trained in the accounting and financial disciplines can learn to be good planners. Nonfinancial managers, those people who come from disciplines other than finance, usually make terrific planners because they have learned through experience to look at many facets of a problem, to take a more general view. But sometimes, buried deep in their psyche, is the fear that they may not do everything well because they lack that formal financial training.

This chapter and the checklist below are a reminder to all planners that there is no mystery to finance; it is simply another tool for the orderly, back-to-basics planning and management process to which you are committed.

Financial planning is a matter of attitude—a positive attitude. It involves understanding every aspect of planning and management so that you always have the opportunity to say yes. You can take a large stride toward being able to say yes by familiarizing yourself with the following key financial and budgeting concepts:

- Financial statements exist to
  Record
  Measure
  Project
- Financial statements exist to answer the question, "How are we doing?"
- Financial reports contain data on
  Revenues
  Costs
  Profits or losses
  Company assets
  Company liabilities

- The term revenues refers to all the income an enterprise generates.
- Costs are incurred by all businesses and are generally categorized as
  Fixed costs
  Variable costs
- *Controllable* and *noncontrollable costs* are not accounting terms; rather, they signify the potential of managerial decision making to vary costs.
- Pearl Bailey said once, "I've been rich and I've been poor. Rich is better." The bottom line: Profits (the difference between revenues and costs) are better.
- Return on investment (ROI) is the statistical measurement of the progress of a company; generally speaking, the ROI figure is arrived at by dividing earnings by total investment.
- Assets are the resources that a business owns.
- Liabilities are obligations owed by the business to persons or businesses other than its owners.
- Owners' equity is what the business owes its owners (stockholders).
- Therefore, a balance sheet is a numerical statement of the following formula: Assets = liabilities + owners' equity.
- Current assets can reasonably be expected to be converted to cash or consumed promptly. Fixed assets are expected to last longer and are usually depreciated over a period of time. "Other" assets are those that don't fit into the foregoing two categories.
- Current liabilities are obligations payable in the current fiscal period. Long-term liabilities are payable later than the current period.
- You can analyze a balance sheet using one of two formulas:

$$\text{Current ratio} = \frac{\text{Current assets}}{\text{current liabilities}}$$

$$\text{Working capital} = \text{current assets} - \text{current liabilities}$$

- The funds-flow statement shows the movement of funds through a business over a period of time, including earnings, loans, stock sales, sales of assets, repayment of debt and distribution of dividends.

- Performance statistics allow managers to compare various aspects of the business on a percentage basis. Such statistics becomes a handy tool for the management of progress.

7 THE PLANNING OUTLINE

"To gild refined gold, to paint the lily...is wasteful and ridiculous excess."
—William Shakespeare, King John, IV, ii, II

The back-to-basics plan for a department, a division or a company can be as long or as short as the needs of the venture dictate. If the written narrative answers all the questions a reviewer has, then it's long enough, even if it consists of only two pages. If there are unanswered questions or fuzzy thinking, 50 pages won't make a difference.

However, an *outline* of the plan's requirements makes life easier, both for the manager writing the plan and for the person reviewing it and consolidating it with other plans.

Let us state again that there is *no* universally best format for writing a business plan. However, in our experience, the following back-to-basics planning outline, developed from years of experience in a number of companies, is a very serviceable tool that gets the process started, particularly in firms where formalized planning is a new activity. We have found that if this back-to-basics outline is followed, it answers most of the questions that crop up during the planning and review process.

For definitions of each element of the plan, review Chapter 2 ("The Planning Process"). If you choose to use the following material to develop a planning guide, or suggested format, for your managers to follow, you might wish to include a copy of the definitions of the plan's elements as well, so that each manager will be working from the same premise.

Figure 7.1
Assumptions

19___ PLAN

Dept. name: _____   Prepared by: _____
Dept. number: _____   Date prepared: _____

THE COMPANY'S ECONOMIC ASSUMPTIONS ABOUT 19___ COSTS
Salaries   _____% increase
Bonuses   _____% increase
Commissions   _____% increase
Telephone
Travel and entertainment
Inflation rate
Rent increases
Cost of goods increases
Industry trends

THE MANAGER'S ASSUMPTIONS
Identify those items in your area that will have statistical or economic impact in the coming year and that have guided you in your planning and budgeting process.

Figure 7.2
Project

19___ PLAN

Dept. name: _____   Prepared by: _____
Dept. number: _____   Date prepared: _____

MISSION

FUNCTION

Figure 7.3
Overview

19__ PLAN

Dept. name: _____   Prepared by: _____
Dept. number: _____   Date prepared:

ENVIRONMENT

Economic

Cultural/Social

Political

Demographic

Tehnological

Artistic/Development

Internal

BUSINESS

Critical Success Factors

Competitive Position

Trends/Industry Developments

Strengths

Weaknesses

FUTURE

Major Opportunities

Major Threats

Figure 7.4
Operating Plan

19__ PLAN

Dept. name: _____   *Prepared by:* _____

Dept. number: _____   *Date prepared:* _____

OBJECTIVES

STRATEGIES

CRITICAL FACTORS

Figure 7.5
Plan Summary

19__ PLAN

Dept. name: _____   Prepared by: _____
Dept. number: _____   Date prepared: _____

REVENUE

	1st Qtr.	2d Qtr.	3d Qtr.	4th Qtr.	Total
Gross					
Net					
Profit	_____	_____	_____	_____	_____

DETAIL

	Jan.	Feb.	Mar.	1st Qtr.	2d Qtr.	3d Qtr.	4th Qtr.	Total
TOTAL								

Figure 7.6
Departmental Operations: Narrative

19__ PLAN

Dept. name: _____   Prepared by: _____
Dept. number: _____   Date prepared: _____

Figure 7.7
New Projects[1]

19__ PLAN

Dept. name: _____   Prepared by: _____
Dept. number: _____   Date prepared: _____

DESCRIPTION OF NEW PROJECT

OJBECTIVES OF NEW PROJECT

COST OF NEW PROJECT
Resources Required—19__

	1st Qtr.	2d Qtr.	3d Qtr.	4th Qtr.	Total
Personnel (no. of people)[2]					
Capital purchases ($)[3]					

Budgeted Expenses

Salary
Travel
Entertainment
Telephone
Supplies/stock
Research data
Leased equipment
Rent/space allocation
Other: _____
_____

TOTAL

[1]Use a separate page for each new project.
[2]On a separate sheet, indicate job title, a brief description of duties, justification and proposed salary.
[3]This should agree with your original capital purchase request.

Figure 7.8
Alternate Plans

19__ PLAN

Dept. name: _____   Prepared by: _____
Dept. number: _____   Date prepared: _____

NARRATIVE

Figure 7.9
Alternate Plans

19__ PLAN

Dept. name: _____   Prepared by: _____
Dept. number: _____   Date prepared: _____

TOTAL CONTROLLABLE COSTS PER PLAN SUBMISSION $ _____

ALTERNATE PLAN LEVELS

                                          5% of Above   *10% of Above*

Total reduction   _____   _____

Details of total reduction

     1. _____
     2. _____
     3. _____
     4. _____
     5. _____
     6. _____
     7. _____
     8. _____
     9. _____
    10. _____
    11. _____
    12. _____

     TOTAL (must equal total   _____   _____
     reduction)

COMMENTS (IF ANY)

Figure 7.10
Action Plans

19___ PLAN

Dept. name: _____
Dept. number: _____

Prepared by: _____
Date prepared: _____

Code No.	Date Assigned	Program (Objective)	Responsibility	Budget	Due Date	Date Reviewed	Status

Figure 7.11
Financial History

Dept. name: _____
Dept. number: _____

Prepared by: _____
Date prepared: _____

19___ PLAN

	19__	19__	19__	19__	Current Year	Next Year	19__	19__	19__	19__	19__
Revenues											
Expenses											
Profit/(loss)											
Profit margin (%)											
Share of market											

Figure 7.12
Resource Requirements (Capital Budget Requests)

19___ PLAN

Dept. name: _____
Dept. number: _____

Prepared by: _____
Date prepared: _____

Project No.	Project Description	Total Project Cost	Cash Paid Prior to End of Year	Estimated Timing of Cash Expenditures							
				Next Year				Year Total	19___ Year Total	19___ Year Total	19___ Year Total
				1st Qtr.	2d Qtr.	3d Qtr.	4th Qtr.				

Division Management Approval _____

Figure 7.13
Long-Range Plans

19___ PLAN

Dept. name: _____   Prepared by: _____
Dept. number: _____   Date prepared: _____

NARRATIVE

DETAIL

	Next Year	19___	19___	19___	19___
Head Count					
Salaried					
Hourly					
Union					
Commission					
Other	_____	_____	_____	_____	_____
TOTAL	======	======	======	======	======
New Positions (List)[1]					
Projected Revenues	_____	_____	_____	_____	_____

[1] Indicate number per year; also, on a separate sheet, indicate job titles and provide a brief description of duties, justification and salaries for added personnel.

Total
Controllable Costs

    Salary expense
    Travel expense
    Entertainment
    Telephone
    Supplies/Stock
    Research data
    Leased equipment
    Rent/space
      allocation
    Other: _____

_____

    SUBTOTAL

New projects (description/
    cost) (include equipment
    purchase)

    TOTAL

    Projected Profits

Figure 7.14
Head Count

19__ PLAN

Dept. name: _____
Dept. number: _____

Prepared by: _____
Date prepared: _____

	19__	19__	19__	Current Year	Next Year	19__	19__	19__	19__
Location									
Salaried Hourly									
Union									
Commissioned									
Part-time									
(etc.)									

CHECKLIST FOR THE PLANNING OUTLINE
"Touch all the bases."

Although there is no such thing as a universal planning form, the fact is that a specialized planning form, devised to satisfy the unique requirements of a particular company and used by all the firm's planning managers, enables all of them to "speak the same language."

It facilitates internal communication and provides the outside world with a coherent view of the venture's destiny.

Put more simply, the back-to-basics planning outline *works*. It can be longer or more elaborate, as your own needs dictate. But generally speaking, it should not be shorter. All the issues we mention are issues you need to address in order to "touch all the bases." As with every good outline, it prevents you from forgetting important elements.

The following points are reminders as you begin preparing a back-to-basics planning outline.

- If everyone follows the same form, it's easier to analyze, consolidate, review and alter the finished product.

- If the company issues economic assumptions on certain topics, all the plans will be easier to compare and consolidate.

- When you prepare your "New Projects" plan, remember to use one page per project and fill out all the information. The more you tell management, the more likely you are to be understood *and* to get approval.

- The "Alternate Plan" pages give you control of what budget items might be cut rather than relying on management's understanding of your department. Be open and honest when you fill out this section.

- Your "Long-Range Plans" should be vision, not fantasy; achievable, not wishful thinking; based on facts and trends, not on hope.

- "Action Plans" are the primary tools you will use on a day-to-day basis to manage your responsibilities, direct your staff, achieve your goals. Spend the time necessary to put them into place, and monitor, monitor, monitor!

- Your capital budget request ("Resource Requirements") should be prepared with care and a great deal of thought. After all, the future of your venture is at stake!

8 THE BACK-TO-BASICS PLANNER

"Don't put off until tomorrow what you can do today."

Everybody should be a planner—the elevator operator, the supervisor of the custodial staff, the sales manager, the director of administration, the president.

Those who hire planners miss the point. Our premise is that planning is inseparable from every activity, particularly in business. Planning that is separate from the operation is planning in limbo and is therefore wishful thinking. Business conducted without planning is business at risk and is likewise wishful thinking.

Planning is basic, integral, generic and fundamental. Everyone is a planner—like it or not, for better or worse.

We have tried to identify in this book many of those basic principles, garnered from years of planning, management, observation, reading and hard work. We promised you a "how-to" book, and we sincerely hope we have succeeded in inspiring you—not just to make the effort involved but to achieve the reward that good, back-to-basics planning can bring. It's always more fun to look forward, toward the future, than in any other direction. Planners look forward.

CHARACTERISTICS OF THE PLANNER

After reviewing the foregoing material, we discussed what kind of approach we should use in the final chapter. Since we have already given you "checklists" for every aspect of your business plan, it seemed redundant to summarize the things you are going to *do*. But it did seem exciting to discuss the kind of person you're going to *be* as a back-to-basics planner.

When asked "What do you want to be when you grow up?" most children will answer, "an astronaut," "a lawyer," "a fire fighter," "a tennis player," "an opera star"—those visible, well-rewarded careers that become the role models for girls and boys as they grow up. Wouldn't it be wonderful if the children of the future said without hesitation, "a planner." My! What a world of potential that opens up! All careers, all goals, all happiness are possible with those two words. With that enthusiasm driving us, we reread the manuscript and looked for those *characteristics* that define the back-to-basics planner.

Upon reviewing the list of characteristics, it became obvious to us that many of them are present in successful people in a wide range of fields. But it seems to us that the *combination* of characteristics defines a very special person. We offer that list for your consideration:

Curiosity	Dedication
Integrity	Verbal, oral, writing skills
Vision/imagination	Hard work
Respect for others	Agility
Loyalty	Personal best
Ambition	

Curiosity

Education is the beginning. We do not wish to launch a discussion of the American educational system. We would rather discuss a very personal view of the definition of education. It is not a process of draining the knowledge from one person (the "teacher") into the brain of another person (the "student") and then having that student feed back the information, through tests or other means, for a reward. Education is a process of discovery. At its best, a person finds out through education that there is something to learn, that multiple means (including personal endeavor and exploration) exist to discover those facts and ideas, and that education is therefore the adventure of a lifetime. While we would not suggest that Chekhov's "perpetual student" was an ideal character in *The Cherry Orchard*, ceaseless curiosity in a constantly changing world is the most exciting adventure of all—an adventure of the mind.

A planner is curious, because the status quo is unacceptable (since it is impossible). The fundamental characteristic of back-to-basics planners, given the task they accept, seems to us to be *curiosity*, about all the things they are interested in—and all the things they are not.

Integrity

It is worth repeating that the companies that constantly win the accolades of their peers and competitors as the "best" are generally run with personal and corporate integrity.

Webster defines the term *integrity* as "completeness, wholeness, unimpaired condition, soundness, honesty, sincerity." Those words embody a philosophy that a person or a company could embrace.

Personal and company integrity should be in sync. The good back-to-basics planner realizes early on that the standards of a company and of the individuals within that company must not be in conflict or the future is hopeless.

A favorite aphorism holds that "Good guys finish last." Facts do not support the saying. Despite all the "bad news" with which we're bombarded every day, careful analysis discloses that honesty, soundness, sincerity, wholeness do make a difference. The surveys of successful companies substantiate this claim. Personal integrity shows up regularly in the basic human equation. To put it in the boldest terms, in a world that could have destroyed itself at any time over the past 40 years, 158 nations now exist where there were 51 in 1945; the democratic/parliamentary system far outweighs all other forms of government; all cultures cooperate in the battle against disease and hunger; individuals continue every day to aid their fellow humans; and personal philanthropy still accounts for 85 percent of all giving in the Western world. Good guys finish first.

Vision/Imagination

Like Plato, the back-to-basics planner dreams of the world that can be. On a more mundane level, what was the world like before the paper clip? Wouldn't you like to have invented it?

As we said in the chapter on marketing, every good plan begins with an *idea*. Ideas take imagination, the ability to envision something that does not yet exist. It is a gift that most children have, and as we grow older, the ability is suppressed for an assortment of reasons. Perhaps we do not want to be "different."

But a good planner realizes that different is not bad (nor is it necessarily good—but it does offer a new possibility). A good planner has ideas, encourages ideas, discovers ideas. A good planner creates the environment in which ideas flourish and in which, even when ideas are rejected, the participants keep coming back with more. Remember, "You never know where a good idea will come from."

Respect for Others

In the 1970s there was considerable discussion about the difference between an "aggressive" and an "assertive" person. The consensus finally arrived at was that an aggressive person is concerned with himself or herself, while an assertive person takes into consideration the feelings of others while working to achieve his or her goals.

Respect means to show esteem, consideration or regard for others. Remember our chapter on quantifying. Unless there is communication, such tasks as planning, management and budgeting are nearly impossible. Communication begins with respect—mutual respect. A good back-to-basics planner knows he or she has to *get* it, has to *give* it and has to *keep* it.

Will Rogers said years ago, "I never met a man I didn't like." A boss answered years later, "He never met some of the people I've worked for!" Well, we don't have to like everyone. But we start by listening and trying to understand—that is, we start with respect. We also have to realize that some things—or some people—are impossible. But all are worth a try.

Loyalty

"These are the times that try men's souls. The summer soldier and the sunshine patriot will, in this crisis, shrink from the service of their country." With those words, Thomas Paine made his case for loyalty—a loyalty that goes beyond good times and fair weather, a loyalty that digs in and gets busy when the going gets tough. The last thing any venture needs in times of adversity is the fleeing heels of the fainthearted.

"A poor thing, but mine own" is hardly the slogan for a back-to-basics planner. A tendency to flee in the face of competition, hard times, bad judgment, changing situations is absolutely *not* one of the characteristics of a successful planner, a successful company, a successful person.

Loyalty—not blind loyalty in the face of venality and disaster, but informed loyalty to the venture, its future, its options—is one of the most admirable traits in any human endeavor. It must be counted among the characteristics of a good planner—because if the work is done well, a turnaround is always possible.

Ambition

In the past decade, many words have fallen into disrepute. One is *power*; another is *ambition*. We are supposed to be ambitious, but we're not supposed to *show* it. Even Webster displays some ambiguity in its definition: Ambition is said to mean "strong desire for fame"; while ambitious is defined as "showing great effort."

Although it may be possible to achieve fame without effort, it's hard to think of an example. Good back-to-basics planners are inevitably looking for recognition in their environment (remember what we said in the Introduction about making yourself visible?), but it is unlikely to come about without effort.

The characteristic of good planners is that they are, quite frankly, willing to *exert themselves*—to make that extra effort that will help the venture be successful and (incidentally) help them achieve recognition.

Like *power*, *recognition* is *not* a bad word; it becomes one only through the manner in which it is used. A good planner knows that the success of any venture means that many people were involved, so there must be enough recognition (and reward) to go around.

One is reminded of the television classic "Marty," in which the constant question was, "What do *you* want to do, Marty?" A good planner *knows* what he or she wants to do, and some people call that ambition.

Dedication

There is a wonderful story, quite possibly apochryphal, that demonstrates dedication at its most remarkable. Meredith Willson was a piccolo player, composer and conductor with a solid career in music and broadcasting. In the 1950s he wrote a show based on his boyhood in Iowa. It was called *The Music Man*. The story goes that he and his wife gave over 100 auditions of the musical to prospective producers but struck out with all of them. Finally, their luck turned. Kermit Bloomgarten was the one who didn't say, "Who wants to see a show about a music instrument salesman at the turn of the century?" He produced the show, and the rest, as they say, is theatrical history. Nearly *everyone* wanted to see it.

That's dedication. Some people might point out that Mr. Willson was dedicated to his *own* creation. But then, a good back-to-basics planner is likewise dedicated to ideas that are his or hers or that are—in the very best cases—the mutual ideas of the group.

Dedication to the objectives of the venture is surely a necessary characteristic of a good planner. It's easy to go with a winner; what is needed is the flag waver, the bugle blower, the believer, to see the project over the hard spots and *create* that winner.

Verbal, Oral, Writing Skills

Let's start with some definitions. How many of you confuse the use of the words *verbal* and *oral*? We will say, "She has great verbal ability," when we mean that she speaks well. What we should say is, "She has great oral ability." *Verbal* means an understanding and good use of words; *oral* refers to our speaking ability. Of course, writing skills are also necessary for the back-to-basics planner.

We have indicated often in this book that plans must be written to be useful. Obviously, this implies that they must be written well.

In most companies it is also necessary that the plan be *presented.* Many times, the quality of that presentation can spell the difference between acceptance or rejection of the plan. That may seem unfair, but that's the way it is.

So a good planner is a good writer, able to express ideas succinctly, imaginatively and convincingly. He or she must be able to present those plans—in a truncated form, if necessary—with the proper choice of words (verbal skills) and in a pleasing and convincing manner (oral skills).

If you don't have these skills, learn them. Sometimes they *can* make the difference.

Hard Work

The last time we visited Menlo Park in New Jersey, we were told that Thomas Alva Edison owned the most patents ever granted by the United States government. It is doubtful that the statistic has changed since then. It is a remarkable experience to visit the laboratory and factory of the "genius of Menlo Park." All one has to see is the first light bulb, the first phonograph and the first motion picture studio to get some understanding of Edison's productivity and creativity. He is known as a great inventor and a great *innovator* (in the cultural sense of that word).

However, one of his best-known quotes is, "My work is 10 percent inspiration and 90 percent perspiration."

There is little else to add to that equation.

Agility

Robert Frost wrote a poem called "The Road Not Taken," in which he followed the path "less traveled by"—concluding that choice "has made all the difference."

A good planner often goes down the road "less traveled by" others, when he or she is breaking new ground, charting new courses; and that, indeed, can make "all the difference."

We have talked about vision in analyzing the future, looking objectively at the critical factors, devising alternate plans for the success of the venture. This takes agility, the ability to react quickly and effectively in a crisis or an unpredictable situation.

Personal Best

Students of history know that the survival of civilization sometimes rests on the eloquence of a single person. In the darkest days of Hitler's conquest of Europe, before America's entry into World War II, one man stood alone, with little more than audacity and the skill of the English language, to summon the impossible—the personal best—from the generations at risk. We speak, of course, of Winston Churchill.

While the above paragraph may simplify the political/military complexities of the situation, judgment must linger on the facts. Germany had overrun all of Europe and had a military machine more devastating than any in history. Students of statistics and many "seers" wrote off England and urged America to make accommodations with the Third Reich.

Churchill summoned—from some unknown source—the will, the courage, the resources to prevail.

How do we define personal best? That indescribable something that inspires, leads, serves as an example. Fate willing, none of us will ever have to play a role such as Churchill's, and the survival of civilization will not depend upon our individual effort. But those who reach deep inside themselves for the best that is within them *can* prevail—and better still, succeed. This cannot be taught. But without a doubt, it can be summoned. It can come from some remarkable source; and if we seek, we can find it within ourselves. The best planners, the best managers, the real achievers dig a little deeper, plumb unknown depths and find that extra strength to *pull together all the other characteristics* into a winning formula.

EPILOGUE

We have come full circle. We asked in the Introduction, *"What makes the difference between good or adequate individuals and organizations and great ones?"* We cited values as the paramount difference. And we offered back-to-basics planning as the first step toward making up that difference.

We have attempted to give you both the tools to initiate back-to-basics planning and the *reasons* for using those tools. For when the proper tools are knowledgeably utilized in any planning effort, the payoff for the back-to-basics planner is outstanding performance.

SELECTED READING

Abell, Derek F.; and Hammond, John S. *Strategic Market Planning.* Englewood Cliffs, N.J.: Prentice-Hall, 1979.

Ansoff, H. Igor. *Strategy Plus Structure Equals Performance.* Edited by Hans B. Thorelli. Bloomington, Ind.: Indiana University Press, 1977.

Berry, Dick. *Industrial Marketing for Results.* Reading, Mass.: Addison-Wesley Publishing Co., 1981.

Boston Consulting Group. *Perspective on Experience.* Boston: The Boston Consulting Group, 1972.

Brion, John M. *Corporate Marketing Planning.* New York: John Wiley & Sons, 1967.

Campbell, John F. *Managerial Behavior, Performance and Effectiveness.* New York: McGraw-Hill, 1970.

"Competitive Analysis." The Hayes-Hill Report 12. Prepared by Hayes-Hill Management Consultants. Chicago, Ill: April 1981.

Coop, Robert; *Strengthening Employee Performance Evaluation*. Chicago, Ill.: Public Personnel Association, 1966.

Cooper, Caryl. *Improving Interpersonal Relations*. Englewood Cliffs, N.J.: Prentice-Hall, 1982.

Cooper, Joseph D. *How to Get More Done in Less Time*. Garden City, N.Y.: Doubleday, 1962

Corbin, Arnold. "Using a Team Approach to Market-Oriented Planning." *Management Review* (June 1977). pp. 9-15.

Crosby, Philip B. *The Art of Getting Your Own Sweet Way*. New York: McGraw-Hill, 1974.

Culligan, Matthew J.; Deakins, C. Suzanne; and Young, Arthur H. *Back-to-Basics Management*. New York: Facts On File, 1983.

Dickson, Paul. *The Future File: A Guide for People with One Foot in the Twenty-First Century*. New York: Rawson Associates, 1977.

Dowling, William F. Jr.; and Sayles, Leonard R. *How Managers Motivate: The Imperatives of Supervision*. New York: McGraw-Hill, 1978.

Drucker, Peter F. *Managing in Turbulent Times*. New York: Harper & Row, 1980.

————*Management: Tasks, Practices, Reponsibilities*. New York: Harper & Row, Publishers, 1973.

————*The Practice of Management*. New York: Harper & Row, 1954.

————*Managing for Results*. New York: Harper & Row, 1964.

————*The Effective Executive*. New York: Harper & Row, 1966.

Haas, Robert. *Industrial Marketing Management*. New York: Petrocelli/Charter, 1976.

Hax, Arnoldo C.; and Majluf, Nicolas S. *A Methodological Approach for the Developing of Strategic Planning in Diversified Corporations.* Tech Report 3. Cambridge, Mass.: Sloan School of Management, M.I.T. August 1977.

————*Towards the Formalization of Strategic Planning—A Conceptual Approach.* Tech Report 2. Cambridge, Mass.: Sloan School of Management, M.I.T. August 1977.

Heilbroner, Robert L.; et al. *In the Name of Profit: Profiles in Corporate Irresponsibility.* Garden City, N.Y.: Doubleday, 1972.

Hennessy, J.H., Jr. *Acquiring and Merging Businesses.* Englewood Cliffs, N.J.: Prentice-Hall, 1966.

Hill, Richard M.; Alexander, Ralph S.; and Cross, James S. *Industrial Marketing.* Homewood, Ill.: Richard D. Irwin, 1975.

Hofer, Charles W.; and Schendel, Dan. *Strategy Formulation: Analytical Concepts.* St. Paul, Minn.: West Publishing, 1978.

Hurd, Douglas A. *Vulnerability Analysis in Business Planning.* Research Report 593. Menlo Park, Calif.: SRI International, 1977.

Kastens, Merritt L. *Long-Range Planning for Your Business.* New York: AMACOM, 1976.

Koontz, Harold. *Appraising Managers as Managers.* New York: McGraw-Hill, 1971.

Kurtz, David L.; and Boone, Louis E. *Marketing.* Hinsdale, Ill.: The Dryden Press, 1981.

Levin, Richard; and Iamone, Rudolph P. *Quantitative Disciplines in Management Decisions.* Belmont, Calif.: Dickenson Pub. Co., 1969.

Lipper, Arthur III. *Investing in Private Companies.* Homewood, Ill.: Dow Jones-Irwin, 1984.

Lorange, Peter; and Vancil, Richard F. *Strategic Planning Systems.* Englewood Cliffs, N.J.: Prentice-Hall, 1977.

Love, Sydney F. *Mastery and Management of Time.* Englewood Cliffs, N.J.: Prentice-Hall, 1978.

Maher, John R. *New Perspectives in Job Enrichment.* New York: Van Nostrand Reinhold Co., 1971.

Maslow, A. H. *Motivation and Personality.* New York: Harper & Row, 1954.

Miller, Ernest C. *Marketing/Planning Approaches of Selected Companies.* Research Study 81. New York: American Management Association, 1967.

———*Objectives and Standards: An Approach to Planning and Control.* Research Study 72. New York: American Management Association, 1966.

———*Objectives and Standards of Performance in Financial Management.* Research Study 87. New York: American Management Association, 1968.

———*Objectives and Standards of Performance in Production Management.* Research Study 84. New York: American Management Association, 1967.

Moose, Sandra O. "Barriers and Umbrellas." Perspectives of the Boston Consulting Group, no. 232, 1980.

Naisbitt, John. *Megatrends.* New York: Warner Books, 1982.

Naylor, Thomas H. *Strategic Planning Management.* Oxford, Ohio: Planning Executives' Institute, 1980.

O'Connor, Rochelle. *Planning under Uncertainty: Multiple Scenarios and Contingency Planning.* Conference Board Report 741. New York: 1978.

O'Dell, William F.; Ruppel, Andrew C.; and Trent, Robert H. *Marketing Decision Making: Analytical Framework and Cases.* Cincinnati, Ohio: South-Western Publishing Co., 1976.

"Performance Appraisals: Effects on Employees and Their Performance." Ann Arbor, Mich: Foundation for Research on Human Behavior, University of Michigan, 1963.

Peter, Dr. Laurence J.; and Hull, Raymond. *The Peter Principle.* New York: William Morrow & Company, 1969.

Peters, Thomas J.; and Waterman, Robert H., Jr. *In Search of Excellence*. New York: Harper & Row, 1982.

Porter, Michael E. *Competitive Strategy*. New York: The Free Press, 1980

Quinn, James Brian. "Managing Strategic Change." Sloan Management Review (Summer 1980.) pp. 3-17.

Randolph, Robert M. *Planagement—Moving Concept into Reality*. New York: AMACOM, 1975.

Rausch, Bernard A. *Strategic Marketing Planning*. New York: American Management Association, 1982.

Ries, Al; and Trout, Jack. *Positioning: The Battle for Your Mind*. New York: McGraw-Hill Book Company, 1981.

Robinson, S.J.Q.; Hitchens, R.E.; and Wade, D.P. "The Directional Policy Matrix—Tool for Strategic Planning." Long-Range Planning 11. New York: AMACOM, June 1978. pp. 8-15.

Rowland, Virgil K. *Evaluating and Improving Managerial Performance*. New York: McGraw-Hill, 1970.

Schendel, Dan E.; Hofer, Charles W.; eds. *A New View of Business Policy and Planning*. Boston: Little, Brown & Co., 1979.

Schoeffler, Sidney. "Nine Basic Findings on Business Strategy." Pimsletter no. 1. Cambridge, Mass.: Strategic Planning Institute, 1977.

Strategic Management in General Electric. Fairfield, Conn.: General Electric, 1979.

Trebuss, A. Susanna. *Improving Corporate Effectiveness: Managing the Marketing/Finance Interface*. Montreal: The Conference Board in Canada, 1978.

Uris, Auren; and Noppel, Marjorie. *The Turned-on Executive*. New York: McGraw-Hill, 1970.

Valentine, Raymond F. *Performance Objectives for Managers*. New York: American Management Association, 1966.

Wasson, Chester R. *Dynamic Competitive Strategy and Product Life Cycles.* Austin, Tex.: Austin Press, 1978.

Webber, Ross A. *Time Is Money.* New York: Macmillan, 1980.

Yip, George S. *Barriers to Entry: A Corporate Strategy Perspective.* Cambridge, Mass.: Strategic Planning Institute, 1981.

INDEX